Best of the Best presents

Bob Warden's
Favorite
Ninja Recipes

Press a button and go!

Create delicious recipes that will inspire you to eat and live well!

ANYTIME CRÊPES P 91

Best of the Best presents

Bob Warden's
Favorite
Ninja Recipes

Bob Warden

with Stephen Delaney
and Andrea Schwob

QUAIL RIDGE PRESS
Preserving America's Food Heritage

ISBN 978-1-934193-90-7
Printed in USA
9 8 7 6

Book Development by:
The Culinary Palette, Ronda DiGuglielmo
Land & Associates, Donna Land

Food and product photographs by Karl McWherter

Author photograph by Benoit Cortet

Edited by Gwen McKee and Terresa Ray

Published by Quail Ridge Press
and Great Chefs International

www.quailridge.com
www.greatchefsinternational.com

Contents

SMOOTHIES & SHAKES

SIPPING SENSATIONS

SANDWICHES & SUCH

SASSY SAUCES

BREAKFAST & THE BAKERY

SOUPS & SIDES

DESSERTS & FROZEN TREATS

GO-WITHS

SUN-DRIED TOMATO PESTO   P 76

Foreword by Gwen McKee

Gwen McKee is a cookbook publisher, author, editor, and frequent QVC guest. Her company, Quail Ridge Press, has published over 200 cookbooks.

Most everybody has a blender of some kind in their kitchen. Over the years, I have gone through the kind with buttons that eventually got stuck when something sticky ran down the sides and rendered a few of the speeds useless. When I replaced that one, the next one burned out when the blade got stuck trying to grind something too big for its blade. I eventually graduated to a thick glass one with a much better motor that I was perfectly satisfied with . . . until a few years ago, when my good buddy Bob Warden came to me with a new kind of blending machine.

"Gwennie, you don't know what you're missing till you try this Ninja!"

I looked at him quizzically. "Okay, Mr. Bob. Convince me."

He began with a simple question: "Does your blender have just one blade at the bottom?"

"Of course. They all have blades only at the bottom."

"Well, the Ninja has blades from bottom to top." And with that, he got out a Ninja blade and showed it to me. I have to say I was immediately impressed. With blades that went all up and down the stem, I could see right away that it would not be limited to one cutting place where all the ingredients had a hard time getting to the bottom to wait their turn to be chopped. His turning it showed me that some part of those blades were bound to reach all levels in the blender container . . . as soon as it was turned on.

"This stack of super sharp blades is the newest innovation in high-revolution blending."

Now he had my attention. "Go on."

"Does your blender make ice cream?"

"No."

"Or snow-like ice for snowballs?"

"Of course not."

"Does it grind meat?"

"Actually, trying that broke one of my old blenders."

"Does it knead bread dough?"

"Now, come on, Bob, one machine can't do all that."

"Well, it can, and it does. The Ninja doesn't just make smoothies and drinks. It is a total kitchen system that will make prepping, chopping, grinding, pulverizing, and serving delicious food quicker and easier." And you can all guess what my next words were:

"Show me."

And he did. Since then I have bought Ninjas in various styles and configurations for gifts that I am always thanked profusely for and told, "This gift just keeps on giving."

I make a breakfast smoothie for two of fruits, veggies, yogurt, and juices most every morning for my husband Barney and me to get our day off to a great start. The Ninja makes that easy . . . and these recipes give me new ideas to make my morning smoothies more versatile and delicious.

Being a writer and editor of many, many cookbooks, I encouraged Bob to write a special cookbook featuring recipes utilizing all the Ninja's many features. I think people like to have a recipe to go by so that you know not only the ingredients and the amounts, but the speeds, the times, the amount of pulses, etc.—I know I do. So with his chef's expertise and creative cooking ideas, Bob has done it again. We at Quail Ridge Press are proud to present *Bob Warden's Favorite Ninja Recipes* under our "Best of the Best" banner.

Thanks, Bob. Now I know. It's Ninja-licious!

Gwen McKee

The Ninja Kitchen System

The way we live today pulls us in a hundred directions. Demands on our time and attention never let up. And we pay for being so busy, day in and day out, by settling for beverages and foods that really aren't what we want.

Well, the stresses of daily living aren't going away. But the breakthrough technology that drives your Ninja Kitchen System can take the pressure off, helping you make better, healthier things to eat and drink. The Ninja has all you need to prep hundreds of delicious foods and refreshing drinks you'll love—with the full freshness, flavor and nutrition of every ingredient intact. What's more, you'll do it all with amazing speed and simplicity.

This technology, featuring powerful, high-revolution blending and an innovative stacked array of super sharp blades, was developed to meet real needs in the kitchen. It delivers results unlike anything you've seen before from conventional blenders, juicers, mixers or food processors. With the best functionality of all those devices combined in one powerful unit, the Ninja Kitchen System will change for the better the way you fuel up for your busy day.

In no time, these specialties from the Ninja system—and many more—will be staples at your house.

- Whip up smooth and delicious soft-serve ice cream in just thirty seconds with your favorite frozen fruit and dairy products.

- Turn fresh fruits and vegetables into healthful, flavorful smoothies in no time flat.

- Just as quickly and with the same consistent quality, purée the essentials for hearty soups—from the counter to the saucepan in minutes.

- Crave a frozen drink? The Ninja Kitchen System turns out crystalline, snow-like ice you'll use to mix better margaritas, daiquiris or nonalcoholic drinks than most restaurants serve!

- Make your own safer, leaner ground meats—superb, fine-textured hamburger, chicken or pork. The system is great for turning out savory meatballs and sausages, too.

- Prep perfect dough for great homemade bread and pizzas, cookies, cakes and other baked treats, taking advantage of the Ninja's special attachments just for this purpose.

Each model in the Ninja Kitchen System comes with an array of useful, durable accessories you'll use to process and prepare great selections from soup to nuts and everything in between. We're especially excited—and you will be, too—about the unique single-serving capabilities of the system, as helpful for the specific needs of large families as it is for those who cook and blend for one or two.

We're confident you'll rave about the kitchen-tested recipes in this cookbook. Always remember, though, that the information we share is only a starting point. The versatile capabilities of the system inspire many users to create their own custom drinks and dishes. Use the recipes and techniques in this book to help you get started on the exciting possibilities that await you with your Ninja Kitchen System.

16-ounce
single-serve cup

16-ounce
chopper bowl

40-ounce
bowl

48-ounce
pitcher

The heart of a versatile machine

In several important ways, your Ninja Kitchen System represents the latest in food preparation technology. These brilliantly engineered, precision-built devices are much more capable than ordinary blenders, food processors, choppers, mixers and juice extractors. In fact, they take the place of all those narrow-purpose machines, and even eliminate the need for high-priced power blenders.

Here's an example. The single-serve cup you'll find on some Ninja models spins up to a perfectly regulated 24,000 revolutions per minute, with separate gearing that also lets you work at exactly the right speeds for dough-making and food processing. This versatility directly affects the ease and effectiveness with which you create excellent personal drinks and treats. In each of its models, the Ninja system tackles practically anything your kitchen requires of it, producing the impressively consistent textures and complete blending you expect, time after time.

Take another exclusive feature that separates the Ninja system from other devices. To do the basic work of processing, blending, juicing and mixing, Ninja technology stacks interchangeable four- or six-blade assemblies. (This is where we really live up to our name.)

Conventional blenders and food processors have blades only in the bottom of their bowls. In comparison, the Ninja Kitchen System provides even, sharply cut, consistent processing of all ingredients, at exactly the texture your recipe requires.

The design change is basic, and the effect is revolutionary. This blade array processes the entire contents of the bowl simultaneously and evenly in the entire mixing space. The chopping and blending action is consistent throughout, not plagued by uneven half-mush and half-chopped food—a chronic problem with older units.

To accommodate the volume of food or liquid you're using for any recipe, Ninja Kitchen Systems include blender bowls of various sizes, from 40 to 72 ounces. It's always best to use the smallest bowl that accommodates the ingredients in the recipe; however, any larger size container will work. Some of our units, such as the soon-to-be released Ninja Mega Kitchen System are equipped with bowl-in-bowl processing, enabling you to fit a smaller container into the unit's larger bowl. The insert has its own drive. With a size that's right for the smaller processing job, it provides perfect leak proof results.

When you want to prep for baking, the Ninja Kitchen System becomes the perfect batter or dough maker, complete with dough blades and paddles. We'll tell you more about those tools later.

The accessory set for some units also includes up to four single-serve sixteen-ounce cups. These cups make possible one of the most appealing capabilities of the system—its ability to produce a personal size of complete nutrient juices, creamy shakes, nutritious smoothies, perfect frozen drinks, ice cream and much, much more. You'll appreciate the minimal fuss, simple cleanup—and quick gratification.

Whatever model you've selected, you possess an unmatched food preparation system, one that handles a spectrum of kitchen requirements with a precision born of superb design, engineering and manufacturing. But technical prowess alone isn't the most important part of the story. What counts most is the way the features and capabilities of your Ninja Kitchen System can transform the way you prepare food.

Bottoms up: the easy way to make great drinks

If convenience were the only benefit of your Ninja Kitchen System, it would be such a strong one that you'd never again do complete nutrient juicing, smoothies or frozen mixed drinks any other way.

After all, it's incredibly easy to whip up great drinks with the Ninja system. Because you can start with ingredients right out of the freezer, crisper or fruit bowl, prep time is minimal. You may need to do a little washing, peeling and cutting; some drinks require nothing more than putting ingredients right into the blending bowl. The powerful blending and processing capabilities of the Ninja system mean the drink is ready fast. And cleanup is just as quick and uncomplicated.

But there's so much more to making beverages the Ninja way. For one thing, what your unit does with ice is simply spectacular. Its high speed blades produce a light, fine-grained, almost uniform powder that reminds many people of new-fallen snow. The ground ice isn't melted,

and it isn't spoiled by large, incompletely processed chunks that can spoil your enjoyment of the drink.

On the ski slopes, light snow crystals like this are called champagne powder. In your kitchen, you'll call them the best start you've ever seen for a frozen Margarita, Mojito, Bloody Mary, Martini, Cosmopolitan, Piña Colada, Daiquiri or Kamikaze. You and your guests will find these smooth, cold, wonderfully drinkable cocktails better than what you're accustomed to in restaurants and resorts.

Besides a generous selection of frozen mixed drinks, our "Sipping Sensations" chapter features directions for unusual iced sangría that's a delightful complement to paella, chili, burgers or steaks. You'll also want to try our nonalcoholic Sensations, including the ultra healthy Lean Mean & Green, as fresh and flavorful with its grape, kiwi and pear ingredients as it is nutritious.

The exceptional quality of the snow your unit produces may inspire you to invent new drinks. With or without alcohol, they're destined to become regular entries in your mixology repertoire. And keep in mind that it takes only a few squirts of flavored syrup to turn this snow into a summer treat that kids really enjoy.

Of course, most people don't want a frozen cocktail every day of the year. You'll find entries in our "Smoothies and Shakes" chapter that probably will become daily-use staples. They're great tasting, it's true, with rich, satisfying consistencies. But they also pack a potent nutritional punch.

You get the maximum natural benefits of raw super foods from the fresh ingredients found in most of these smoothies. You're tanking up on vitamins, minerals, antioxidants, protein and other essential nutrients. Because complete nutrient juicing does not remove dietary fiber, you're getting new, slowly released energy that makes you feel sharp mentally without spiking your glucose level. And you're doing it all with something that seems more like a treat than a nutrition drink. Simply put, Ninja delivers complete nutrient juicing.

The notion that it's a kind of punishment to have what's good for you won't survive your taste-tests of these recipes. The flavors and textures you'll experience will keep you coming back for more.

We've included some smoothie entries that help you address very particular health needs. Try "Go-To-For-The-Flu" Smoothie (when you think you might be coming down with something) or Detox in the Morning Smoothie (a welcome day-after-the-night-before restorer and pick-me-up).

If what you're really craving is a little indulgence, flip to the section on shakes. For anyone brought up in the United States, the milkshake is an iconic comfort drink. Our section features some delightful takes on classics, like the Old-Fashioned Malted Milkshake, but it'll also turn you on to some eye-opening new ideas. We especially recommend the Strawberry Cheesecake Milkshake and a one-of-a-kind breakfast goodie, the Caramel Waffle Milkshake. ❖

The Sandwich Board

It's been estimated that Americans eat about 45 billion sandwiches a year. (You may feel that you and your family account for about a quarter of that number.) In any case, when we consume so many of these simple meals, it's a pity to settle for the dull turkey-on-rye and tuna-salad-on-whole-wheat types that seem to show up on our plates again and again.

Every model in the Ninja Kitchen System line provides an antidote to boring sandwiches. Check out our "Sandwiches and Such" section for sixteen great ideas that can perk up a lunch—or even a dinner—without a huge investment in time and effort.

Some sandwiches among our recipes will sound familiar. One example is the old reliable ham-and-cheese—but what you get with this one is nothing like the old lunch-counter standby. Ours is a hot sandwich, with a ham, provolone and mayo filling accented by ripe olives, Italian seasoning, red wine vinegar and black pepper. This one gives you an unexpected zing. You may never think of ham and cheese the same way again.

Notice that the spreads you prepare with your Ninja unit are not reduced to undifferentiated goo. Your Ninja's fingertip pulse control works wonders. It enables you to create fillings that live up to their "salad" billing, with the ingredients processed only to the proper consistency, so that individual textures and flavors are preserved.

"Sandwiches and Such" also shows you how to take advantage of the Ninja system's high-tech capabilities to produce excellent ground meats. That's the essential beginning of juicy and flavorful tuna burgers, turkey burgers, veggie bean burgers and classic bacon cheddar burgers. You'll also find two recipes for easy and savory sausage: sweet Italian and chicken apple. ❖

Saucy Selections

In our "Sassy Sauces" chapter, you'll find a spectrum of uses, tastes and textures. We're using the word "sauces" in the broadest possible way here. There are easy-to-follow recipes for salad dressings, dips, marinades, meat rubs, pizza and Alfredo sauces and much more.

Our selections are guided in part by versatility. With the recipes you find here, you'll be able to create dressings and sauces that mingle perfectly with practically any meal you have in mind.

At least as important is our intention to reconcile superb flavors and consistencies with the demands of healthier eating. Many of these entries limit the amount of preser-

vatives, artificial colorings, excess fat and carbohydrates you'll be introducing into your diet. Instead, you will be using fresh fruits, vegetables and herbs without all the chemicals.

Because your Ninja unit helps you produce these delights quickly and without a lot of trouble, you'll find yourself using them often. Because the processor offers pin-point pulse control, you'll discover that you've prepared them exactly as they're meant to be served. It's another example of the many ways that the right equipment—in this case, your Ninja Kitchen System—can help you eat better and enjoy it more. ❖

Baking and Breakfasting

As long as there have been food processors, cooks have used them to prep for baking. But until now, the results have often been disappointing. It's largely a lack of power and control that's to blame. The limitations of previous units made it difficult to get the dough just right. The dough goes into the oven under- or over-worked, and what comes out reflects that. On the one extreme, you get dense, flat loaves that tend to rip when cut. On the other, the bread is dry and crumbly inside with rock-hard crusts.

The Ninja Kitchen System changes all that. It helps you develop glutens properly so you can serve light, moist bread that's just chewy enough. Amazingly, it can achieve the right degree of kneading in as little as twenty seconds.

You can expect similar ease—and consistently excellent results—with the many other baking recipes we've included, from white chocolate macadamia cookies to pizza crusts to sweet pie dough to biscuit batter and much more. Not everything in the baking lineup is breads or sweets; we also feature some savory options, such as our crispy breadsticks and delectable spinach and ricotta pockets. Special attachments including blades and dough paddles will make you a versatile baker. And the tempting treats you'll serve will make you a popular one.

There's no time of day when it's more important to work quickly and efficiently than breakfast, when the day is beckoning and time is often short. Naturally, some of the sweet and delicious recipes we offer in this category can work better as night-before workups or special delights to reserve for weekend brunches. But recipes like our almond waffles or healthy grains pancakes can start the day on time—and with a little extra energy. ❖

Soups and more

In our "Soups and Sides" chapter, you'll find a range of hearty selections we serve on our own tables, dishes of many different origins and characters. They're all refined to make the most of your Ninja system's ability to rapidly process and blend all kinds of ingredients.

Some soups need preliminary chopping; some require the fixings to be puréed. Whatever the specific need, the Ninja's range of functions with perfect pulse control provides the basis of cooking success before you ever put the pot on the stove, getting every aspect of prep work just right.

In keeping with our aim to include dishes that maximize nutrition and keep carbs in check, we offer some true originals, such as loaded cauliflower soup, rich and good without the bulk of potatoes. Or carrot ginger soup, packed with vitamin A and beta carotene, and enlivened with ginger.

The full-flavored sides you'll find in this section provide even more nutritional value. Broccoli patties, pulse-chopped to the desired consistency, win over finicky eaters with an interesting combination of flavors including nutmeg, Swiss cheese and garlic. Our special corn pudding recipe complements almost any main dish with a simple and delicious blend of the sweet and savory. ❖

Go-Withs

As we define it, a go-with is a topping, dip or other complement that finishes any cooked dish or baked treat or snack food—you name it. Go-withs add that extra touch that makes the foods you serve just a little more enjoyable and memorable. We've devised and tested a bunch of them for the Ninja system, and we think you'll be thrilled with the results. Here's a partial list.

The dips: French onion (made fast and easy with real onions, not soup mix), guacamole, hummus and many more. The relishes: onion jam, mango chutney, hot pepper relish and three different salsas. The flavored butters: praline and Mediterranean. Plus special whipped cream variations (so you can make the perfect one for what's under it), a knockout strawberry jam (you may never buy the supermarket kind again), and a can't-miss chocolate mousse (much easier to prepare than others we've seen and tried). ❖

What's for dessert?

Many readers think our chapter on "Desserts and Frozen Treats" should have come first—after all, that's where they'd like to put their favorite course at every meal. Truth is, the order hardly matters. The amazing speed and convenience of the Ninja Kitchen System means you can enjoy a rich, delightful dessert whenever you want it, in not much more time than it takes to think about it.

The most spectacular example is our homemade ice creams and frozen yogurts. These delicious, soft-serve treats are so easy—and, prepared the Ninja way, so good. If you go with our Instant No-Fuss Ice Cream directions, you can be digging in just four minutes after you start. If you're counting calories, you can prepare our Skinny Me Ice Cream variant almost as quickly, and live it up with ice cream that just doesn't taste like it's low in fat and sugar. If you want to shoot the moon,

you can enjoy the fancy custard produced by Our Real Deal Fruit Ice Cream—a luxurious treat that takes a little longer to fix but pays off, we promise, with some of the best ice cream you've ever had.

When you're not in the mood for dairy, plenty of other frozen treats await your pleasure. Our water ice recipes—all of them light, refreshing and low in fat—will keep you coming back for more.

As is true of every category of preparation, there are countless ways to use your Ninja Kitchen System beyond the dessert recipes we've included. Here's a handy tip to keep in mind. If you're going to use a boxed cake mix, prep it with your Ninja unit. As we've timed it, you can be ready to put the batter into the cake pan in ten seconds. If there's a faster and better way to do this common kitchen chore, we've never seen it. ❖

Some final thoughts for top results

For most of our recipes, the fingertip pulse control provided on all Ninja models will help you produce great results as you blend, mix, chop or process any food or beverage. Be guided by the recipes as to how many pulses are needed to achieve the right initial consistency before you process fully. Some recipes are completed using the pulse feature only. As you get accustomed to using the device, your "feel" for best use of the pulse will grow increasingly expert.

Also, keep in mind that our kitchen-tested recipes often specify the sequence in which to add the ingredients. Sticking with this order will yield the best results.

On the first page of this introduction, we mentioned that the Ninja Kitchen System is beautifully suited to experimentation. Many of our recipes encourage you to try substitutions and other new ideas that are cited in the author's tips that accompany most entries. Remember, the possibilities are practically limitless. Make the most of your own favorite tastes and consistencies—and your imagination—to create new drinks and dishes all your own.

The recipes in this book are calculated for use with specific accessories provided with the various Ninja Kitchen System models. Each recipe shows which bowl or cup is intended. At times you may wish to use other size bowls or pitchers than the ones identified in the recipes.

In general, you'll achieve good results by altering amounts in the recipes proportionately to fit the size of the bowl you want to use. You may need to experiment to find the best proportions of ingredients when substituting larger or smaller bowls with any recipe.

Throughout the design, development and manufacturing phases of the Ninja Kitchen System, the well-being of our customers has been a foremost concern. The result is a line of products carefully engineered to be safe in every phase of operation. Don't forget, though, any appliance of this kind relies on sharp blades to do its work. When you set up and when you wash up, take special care as you handle and clean the blades. We also strongly recommend that you rinse the blades thoroughly as soon as possible after every use. By doing so, you'll avoid hard scrubbing to remove dried-on residue from those sharp, hardworking blades.

Finally, we urge you to make the most of the variations in portion size made possible by your Ninja unit. In particular, the sixteen-ounce single-serving cups make it easy to enjoy almost any kind of healthful drink or frozen treat or dessert at almost any time, with surprisingly minimal preparation, processing and clean-up. Once you get in the habit, you'll find yourself enjoying your Ninja Kitchen System every day—at mealtimes, bedtime and any time in between. ❖

Smoothies & Shakes

Smoothies are so popular—these snacks-in-a-glass offer refreshment and nutrition with many bountiful flavors. Hola Granola Smoothie (page 8) even works for breakfast!

With the Ninja, milkshakes are ready in no time. Enjoy childhood favorites like Old-Fashioned Malted Milkshake (page 19) or a new flavor combo in Caramel Waffle Milkshake (page 20).

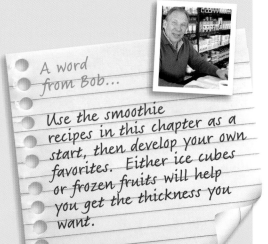

A word from Bob...

Use the smoothie recipes in this chapter as a start, then develop your own favorites. Either ice cubes or frozen fruits will help you get the thickness you want.

Included in this chapter...

Smoothies Solved!

Fresh, fruity smoothies can be a healthful snack or breakfast on the go. You can even freeze them for homemade popsicles! And don't forget to blend in a handful of vitamin-rich greens like spinach or kale! Making a smoothie is easy; start with 1 part liquid, 1 part thickener and 2 parts fruit, then adjust the proportions to your liking.

Below are some component ideas to get you started. Choose one or more from each column to create the flavor combinations that appeal to you: bananas with peanut butter, sweet berries with tart lemonade mix, pumpkin with pumpkin pie spice and honey. Discover your favorite!

Liquid	Thickener	Fruit *Fresh, frozen or canned in juice*	Extras *Add to taste*
Milk, almond milk soy milk, kefir, fruit juice, fruit nectar, coconut milk	Yogurt (regular, Greek, flavored or plain), frozen yogurt, ice cream, sherbet, sorbet, ice	Bananas, strawberries, blueberries, mango, raspberries, cantaloupe, watermelon, pineapple, peaches, canned pumpkin	Peanut butter, chocolate syrup, agave syrup, honey, cinnamon, pumpkin pie spice, nutmeg, sugar-free lemonade mix, fruit preserves

If you start with frozen fruit, you can reduce or omit the thickener, if you like. Remember, smoothies are fun! Start with your favorite fruit (or those on hand in the bottom of your produce drawer) and experiment! To save time in the morning, prep your non-frozen smoothie ingredients and place them in the blender pitcher. Store in the refrigerator overnight. In the morning, add any frozen ingredients, blend and go!

Nuts for Energy Smoothie

Prep: 5 min. **Serves:** 1
16-oz. single-serve cup

I drink this smoothie half an hour before heading to the gym for my afternoon workout to make sure I will have enough energy, protein and carbs to help me endure the two hours of exercise. It also keeps me full until I get home for dinner.—Andrea

Shopping List

¼ cup raisins

⅔ cup soy milk

3 ounces extra firm tofu, cut into ½-inch cubes

1 tablespoon almond butter

¼ teaspoon pure vanilla extract

4 ice cubes

1 Place the raisins and soy milk in the Ninja 16-oz. cup. Screw on blade cap and refrigerate overnight.

2 Add tofu, almond butter, vanilla and ice to the cup. Screw on blade cap.

3 Process for 40 to 45 seconds or until completely smooth.

TIP...
If you don't like soy milk, you can use almond, rice or regular milk.

"Go-To-For-The-Flu" Smoothie

Prep: 2 min. **Serves:** 1
16-oz. single-serve cup

When I get the flu, this is the morning drink that helps me re-cover faster, and it actually tastes good. It has probably all the vita-mins, especially vitamin C, minerals and nutrients.—Stephen

Shopping List

3 ounces frozen raspberries

1½ ounces dried cranberries

2 ounces frozen sliced peaches

½ cup nonfat Greek yogurt

¼ cup orange juice

½ cup peach juice

1 Place raspberries, cranberries, peaches, yogurt and juices in the Ninja 16-oz. cup. Screw on blade cap.

2 Process for 25 to 30 seconds or until completely smooth.

TIP...
You can use only orange juice instead of peach and orange juices if you wish.

Middle Eastern Delight Smoothie

Prep: 6 min. **Serves:** 1
16-oz. single-serve cup

Widely used in the Middle East, dried dates are sweet and full of fiber. Change your smoothie routine and give this unusual drink a try. I am sure it will surprise you.—Bob

Shopping List

2 ounces whole pitted dates

½ cup coconut water

½ banana, peeled

½ cup nonfat Greek yogurt

⅛ teaspoon ground cinnamon

¼ teaspoon pure vanilla extract

3 ice cubes

1 Place dates, coconut water, banana, yogurt, cinnamon, vanilla and ice in the Ninja 16-oz. cup. Screw on blade cap.

2 Process for 40 to 45 seconds or until completely smooth.

TIP...
Any other spices like nutmeg, allspice or even pumpkin pie spice goes great in this drink

Protein Power Smoothie

Prep: 2 min. **Serves:** 1
16-oz. single-serve cup

Great smoothie for after your workout! This gem helps me restore energy in my body and feel great after drinking it. It has lots of fiber, vegetable proteins and good carbs.—Andrea

Shopping List

½ banana, peeled

⅔ cup low-fat (1%) chocolate milk

¼ cup wheat germ

2 tablespoons creamy peanut butter

1 Place banana, milk, wheat germ and peanut butter in the Ninja 16-oz. cup. Screw on blade cap.

2 Process for 20 to 25 seconds or until completely smooth.

TIP...
Switch it up and use ground flaxseed instead of wheat germ from time to time.

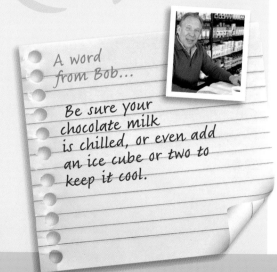

A word from Bob...

Be sure your chocolate milk is chilled, or even add an ice cube or two to keep it cool.

PROTEIN POWER SMOOTHIE

POMEGRANATE BERRY SMOOTHIE

Pomegranate Berry Smoothie

Prep: 2 min. **Serves:** 1
16-oz. single-serve cup

The mix of all the berries with pomegranate juice creates a sweet but tart smoothie. The perfect balance of flavors is great for an afternoon snack.—Stephen

Shopping List

2 ounces frozen raspberries

2 ounces frozen blueberries

2 ounces frozen strawberries

½ cup nonfat Greek yogurt

¾ cup pomegranate juice

1 Place raspberries, blueberries, strawberries, yogurt and juice in the Ninja 16-oz. cup. Screw on blade cap.

2 Process for 25 to 30 seconds or until completely smooth.

TIP...
Keep bags of frozen fruits in the freezer for everyday use in making smoothies!

Detox in the Morning Smoothie

Prep: 2 min. **Serves:** 1
16-oz. single-serve cup

This is my personal choice to have as a breakfast whenever I feel the need to detoxify my body in the morning. Always makes me feel better after I drink it, and it tastes really good.—Andrea

Shopping List

3 ounces frozen strawberries

3 ounces frozen sweet dark cherries

½ cup nonfat Greek yogurt

½ cup acai juice

1 Place strawberries, cherries, yogurt and juice in the Ninja 16-oz. cup. Screw on blade cap.

2 Process for 25 to 30 seconds or until completely smooth.

TIP...
You can use nonfat, vanilla-flavored Greek yogurt for a delicious difference.

Breakfast-With-A-Kick Smoothie

Prep: 4 min. **Serves:** 1
16-oz. single-serve cup

Fruits, vegetables, fiber, antioxidants, vitamins, minerals, vegetable protein, healthy carbs—this smoothie has it all! You won't even know you are drinking such a healthy drink because it tastes delicious.—Stephen

Shopping List

1 pear, peeled, cored and cut into ½-inch pieces

¼ cup almond milk

½ ounce organic watercress

1 piece (1 ounce) cucumber, peeled and seeded

¼ cup acai juice

3 ice cubes

1 Place pear, almond milk, watercress, cucumber, juice and ice in the Ninja 16-oz. cup. Screw on blade cap.

2 Process for 35 to 40 seconds or until completely smooth.

TIP...
If you can't find watercress, use spinach instead.

Hola Granola Smoothie

Prep: 2 min. **Serves:** 1
16-oz. single-serve cup

Yogurt with granola and berries is an excellent healthy breakfast. This smoothie is a great choice when you don't have time to sit down and eat. Just blend it and drink it on the go.—Stephen

Shopping List

¾ cup skim milk

2 tablespoons honey

¼ cup granola

2 ounces frozen blueberries

2 ounces frozen raspberries

½ cup nonfat Greek yogurt

1 Place milk, honey, granola, blueberries, raspberries and yogurt in the Ninja 16-oz. cup. Screw on blade cap.

2 Process 30 to 40 seconds or until completely smooth.

TIP...
Use your favorite cereal instead of granola for a change of pace.

Banana Strawberry Smoothie

Prep: 3 min. **Serves:** 1
16-oz. single-serve cup

You can make the most popular smoothie in the United States right at home using only fresh, natural ingredients.—Bob

Shopping List

½ banana, peeled

4 ounces frozen strawberries

½ cup nonfat Greek yogurt

⅓ cup orange juice

1 Place banana, strawberries, yogurt and orange juice in the Ninja 16-oz. cup. Screw on blade cap.

2 Process 20 to 25 seconds or until completely smooth.

TIP...

Substitute any other frozen fruit for the frozen strawberries.

A word from Bob...

You'll notice that sugar is not needed when you use frozen fruits, with their just-picked peak flavors.

Beautifying My Skin Smoothie

Prep: 2 min. **Serves:** 1
16-oz. single-serve cup

After reading so many magazine articles about foods that are good for your skin, I picked my favorite ones and blended them together. It turned out so good that my friends and I drink this when we get together for an "at home spa day!"—Andrea

Shopping List

6 ounces frozen blueberries

½ banana, peeled and cut into 2 pieces

½ cup nonfat Greek yogurt

¾ cup pomegranate juice

1 Place blueberries, banana, yogurt and juice in the Ninja 16-oz. cup. Screw on blade cap.

2 Process for 25 to 30 seconds or until completely smooth.

TIP...
You can substitute orange, grapefruit or cranberry juice for the pomegranate juice.

Tropical Smoothie

Prep: 6 min. **Serves:** 1
16-oz. single-serve cup

I come from a tropical country, and the usual fruits and fruit juices we have on-hand to make our everyday smoothies are not the same as those in the United States. This smoothie is one of our most popular flavor combinations.—Andrea

Shopping List

2 ounces fresh pineapple chunks

2 ounces fresh papaya chunks

4 ounces fresh mango chunks

¼ cup nonfat Greek yogurt

½ cup passion fruit juice

3 ice cubes

1 Place pineapple, papaya, mango, yogurt, fruit juice and ice in the Ninja 16-oz. single-serve cup. Screw on blade cap.

2 Process for 30 to 35 seconds or until completely smooth.

TIP...
Substitute any fruit of your choice for a smoothie that is all your own.

Peaches and Cherries Smoothie

Prep: 2 min. **Serves:** 1
16-oz. single-serve cup

It is my personal preference that cherries and peaches create a magical combination for use in this drink and many other dishes. Next time you make a peach cobbler, add some fresh pitted cherries to it.—Bob

Shopping List

3 ounces frozen peaches

3 ounces frozen sweet dark cherries

½ cup nonfat Greek yogurt

¼ cup pomegranate juice

½ cup peach juice

1 Place peaches, cherries, yogurt and juices in the Ninja 16-oz. cup. Screw on blade cap.

2 Process for 25 to 30 seconds or until completely smooth.

TIP...

If you can find cherry juice in your local supermarket use it instead of the pomegranate juice for another excellent drink.

Frozen Strawberry Lemonade

Prep: 1 min. **Serves:** 1
16-oz. single-serve cup

Create this popular simple frozen treat without a lot of sugar, preservatives or food colorings. All-natural ingredients help you control what you give your kids to drink.—Stephen

Shopping List

7 frozen strawberries

1⅓ cups lemonade

1 Place strawberries and lemonade in the Ninja 16-oz. cup. Screw on blade cap.

2 Process for 20 to 25 seconds or until well mixed.

TIP...

You can substitute iced tea or your favorite fruit juice for the lemonade.

A word from Bob...

Think about other frozen fruits you might like to substitute—dark sweet cherries, raspberries or blueberries.

STRAWBERRY CHEESECAKE
MILKSHAKE

Strawberry Cheesecake Milkshake

Prep: 4 min. **Serves:** 1
16-oz. single-serve cup

If you are dying for a piece of homemade cheesecake and have no time to bake, try this milkshake which tastes exactly like a cheese-cake topped with fresh strawberries. No oven, no waiting!—Stephen

Shopping List

1 cup strawberry ice cream

2 frozen strawberries

2 ounces cream cheese

¼ teaspoon vanilla extract

⅔ cup whole milk

1 full graham cracker

1 Place ice cream, strawberries, cream cheese, vanilla, milk and cracker in the Ninja 16-oz. cup. Screw on blade cap.

2 Process 15 to 20 seconds or until completely smooth.

TIP...
Substitute any other frozen fruit, such as blue-berries, peaches, raspberries, mango or blackberries for the frozen strawberries.

Chocolate Hazelnut Heaven Milkshake

Prep: 3 min. **Serves:** 1
16-oz. single-serve cup

I can eat the entire jar of the world-famous chocolate hazelnut spread on toast, a croissant, as a dip for fresh fruit or in a crêpe, so how could I not make a milkshake recipe using my little piece of heaven?—Andrea

Shopping List

1½ cups vanilla ice cream

3 tablespoons chocolate hazelnut spread

¼ cup hazelnuts, toasted

¾ cup whole milk

1 Place ice cream, hazelnut spread, hazelnuts and milk in the Ninja 16-oz. cup. Screw on blade cap.

2 Process for 15 to 20 seconds or until well mixed.

TIP...

If you have no time to toast the hazelnuts, just add a little extra chocolate hazelnut spread.

CHOCOLATE HAZELNUT
HEAVEN MILKSHAKE

PUMPKIN PIE MILKSHAKE

Pumpkin Pie Milkshake

Prep: 4 min. **Serves:** 1
16-oz. single-serve cup

*This milkshake is refreshing, and it tastes exactly like having a slice of pumpkin pie. The best part is you can make it just for yourself.
—Stephen*

Shopping List

¼ cup canned pumpkin

½ cup whole milk

⅛ teaspoon ground cinnamon

1 cup vanilla ice cream

¼ teaspoon vanilla extract

⅛ teaspoon ground nutmeg

⅛ teaspoon ground ginger

1 Place pumpkin, milk, cinnamon, ice cream, vanilla, nutmeg and ginger in the Ninja 16-oz. cup. Screw on blade cap.

2 Process for 15 to 20 seconds or until well mixed.

TIP...
Make this milkshake using candied yams instead of the pumpkin.

Banana Crème Pie Milkshake

Prep: 4 min. **Serves:** 1
16-oz. single-serve cup

The local diner makes the best banana cream pie—velvety smooth filling, lots of banana and a perfect vanilla crust! Within minutes I can enjoy those same flavors with this shake.—Andrea

Shopping List

1 banana, peeled, halved

1 cup vanilla ice cream

2 teaspoons vanilla instant pudding mix

8 vanilla wafers

½ cup whole milk

1 Place banana, ice cream, pudding mix, vanilla wafers and milk in the Ninja 16-oz. cup. Screw on blade cap.

2 Process for 15 to 20 seconds or until well mixed.

TIP...
For extra richness, substitute butterscotch instant pudding mix for the vanilla instant pudding mix.

Peanut Butter Cup Milkshake

Prep: 4 min. **Serves:** 1
16-oz. single-serve cup

I remember growing up, trick or treating, and most of my bag was filled with peanut butter cups. It's my personal favorite candy bar and this milkshake really calls it to mind!—Andrea

Shopping List

1 cup vanilla ice cream

2 tablespoons chocolate syrup

1 tablespoon creamy peanut butter

⅓ cup mini peanut butter cups

⅔ cup whole milk

1 Place ice cream, chocolate syrup, peanut butter, peanut butter cups and milk in the Ninja 16-oz. cup. Screw on blade cap.

2 Process for 15 to 20 seconds or until well mixed.

TIP...

If peanut butter is not your thing, you can substitute chocolate-covered wafers, chocolate peppermint patties or your favorite candy bar for the peanut butter cups.

Aloha Milkshake

Prep: 10 min. **Serves:** 1
16-oz. single-serve cup

I always order the same milkshake at my local, very famous, soft-serve ice cream chain. I think my attempt at duplicating it came out pretty close.—Andrea

Shopping List

¼ banana, peeled

⅛ pineapple, peeled and cored

3 tablespoons flaked coconut, toasted

1 cup vanilla ice cream

½ cup whole milk

1 Place banana, pineapple, coconut, ice cream and milk in the Ninja 16-oz. cup. Screw on blade cap.

2 Process for 15 to 20 seconds or until well mixed.

TIP...

If you are in the mood for a milkshake as breakfast, add 1 slice cooked chopped bacon before processing.

Apple Pie Milkshake

Prep: 3 min. **Serves:** 1
16-oz. single-serve cup

If you close your eyes and have a sip of this milkshake, I'll bet you think you're having apple pie à la mode. This indulgence is a lot easier to make!—Bob

Shopping List

1 cup vanilla ice cream

½ cup applesauce

¼ teaspoon cinnamon

¼ cup whole milk

1 Place ice cream, applesauce, cinnamon and milk in the Ninja 16-oz. cup. Screw on blade cap.

2 Process for 10 to 15 seconds or until well mixed.

TIP...
For a holiday take on this shake, add a couple of gingersnap cookies, and process for four more seconds.

A word from Bob...

Make your own apple-sauce by sautéing a few apple slices in butter and cinnamon sugar. Process in your Ninja to the consistency you like.

Old-Fashioned Malted Milkshake

Prep: 2 min. **Serves:** 1
16-oz. single-serve cup

The first malted milkshake in a Chicago drugstore chain in the early 1920's was made with vanilla ice cream, chocolate syrup, milk and malt powder.—Bob

Shopping List

1 cup vanilla ice cream

⅔ cup whole milk

20 chocolate-covered malted milk balls

2 tablespoons chocolate syrup

1 Place ice cream, milk, malted milk balls and chocolate syrup in the Ninja 16-oz. cup. Screw on blade cap.

2 Process for 20 to 25 seconds or until well mixed.

TIP...
This is one milk-shake that goes well with either chocolate or vanilla ice cream.

Chocolate Chocolate Pretzel Milkshake

Prep: 3 min. **Serves:** 1
16-oz. single-serve cup

Pretzels not only satisfy my salty craving but also my sweet craving when I eat them with chocolate. Pretzels add just the right amount of salt to a sweet treat.—Stephen

Shopping List

1 cup chocolate ice cream

¾ cup chocolate milk

¼ cup pretzel twists

⅓ cup mini marshmallows

1 Place the ice cream and milk in the Ninja 16-oz. cup. Screw on blade cap. Process for 10 seconds.

2 Add the pretzels and the mini marshmallows. Screw on the blade cap and process for 6 seconds.

TIP...
This is one of those milk-shakes where you can add almost anything, including nuts, caramel sauce, frozen fruit and chocolate syrup.

Caramel Waffle Milkshake

Prep: 4 min. **Serves:** 1
16-oz. single-serve cup

Breakfast is my favorite meal of the day. I think of it all the time. I wanted to make one of my favor-ite breakfast dishes into a milk-shake.—Andrea

Shopping List

1½ cups vanilla ice cream

2 ounces waffles

2 tablespoons caramel sauce

1 teaspoon maple syrup

⅔ cup whole milk

1 Place ice cream, waffles, caramel sauce, maple syrup and milk in the Ninja 16-oz. cup. Screw on blade cap.

2 Process for 15 to 20 seconds or until well mixed.

TIP...
If you are trying to cut calories, use nonfat or low-fat ingredients instead.

Neapolitan Milkshake

Prep: 3 min. **Serves:** 1
16-oz. single-serve cup

Can't make up your mind if you want a chocolate, strawberry or vanilla milkshake? This recipe has the perfect balance of all three flavors, none overpowered by the other.—Bob

Shopping List

1½ cups strawberry ice cream

⅔ cup whole milk

2 teaspoons vanilla instant pudding mix

1 tablespoon Quick and Easy Chocolate Ganache (page 140), or use chocolate syrup

1 Place ice cream, milk, pudding mix and ganache in the Ninja 16-oz. cup. Screw on blade cap.

2 Process for 15 to 20 seconds or until well mixed.

TIP...
Make it a banana split milkshake by adding ¼ of a peeled banana.

Not-So-Guilty Frozen Coffee

Prep: 5 min. **Serves:** 1
16-oz. single-serve cup

This drink is low in calories with no sugar and no fat. I freeze my left-over coffee into ice cubes, and when I get back home I make myself a delicious guilt-free drink.—Stephen

Shopping List

5 coffee ice cubes

¼ cup coffee

¼ cup sugar-free, fat-free, vanilla-flavored liquid coffee creamer

¼ cup sugar-free, fat-free chocolate syrup

1 To make coffee ice cubes, pour leftover or fresh coffee into ice cube trays and freeze 5 to 6 hours or until frozen completely solid.

2 Place coffee ice cubes, coffee, creamer and chocolate syrup in the Ninja 16-oz. cup. Screw on the blade cap.

3 Process for 35 to 40 seconds or until well mixed.

TIP...
If you don't like liquid coffee creamers, use ¼ cup of any kind of milk mixed with 1 teaspoon sugar or 1 teaspoon sugar substitute.

Sipping Sensations

Frozen drinks are ultra refreshing, especially with the unique flavor combinations here. The Ninja is amazing with ice—see Mocha Russian (page 29) and other alcoholic adult drinks.

You will also love the non-alcoholic drinks in this chapter— extra nutritious foods add great taste, too. Try Market Fresh Boost (page 39), and the fun combo of fruits and vegetables in Red Power Punch (page 36).

A word from Bob...

Never settle for ordinary drinks again! Just add some plain or flavored ice, fresh or frozen fruits or other zesty ingredients, and sipping becomes extraordinary!

Included in this chapter...

Smokin' Hot Mary

Prep: 10 min. **Serves:** 4
**40-oz. bowl or 48-oz. pitcher
with blade attachment**

Traditional Bloody Mary is not served blended, but even when you get creative and blend it with ice, it doesn't lose its flavor and its own characteristics.—Bob

Shopping List

1 celery stalk, cut into 4 pieces

½ lemon, peeled, seeded and cut in half

4 cups ice

⅔ cup vodka

1 cup tomato juice

1 teaspoon ground black pepper

⅛ teaspoon salt

1 tablespoon horseradish

1 teaspoon Worcestershire sauce

8 dashes hot sauce

1 Place celery, lemon, ice, vodka, tomato juice, pepper, salt, horseradish, Worcestershire sauce and hot sauce into the Ninja 40-oz. bowl with blade in position.

2 Process for 50 to 60 seconds or until drink is completely smooth. Carefully remove blade.

TIP...
If you don't like your Bloody Mary spicy, omit the hot sauce and use half the horseradish.

Passion Fruit Mojito

Prep: 8 min. **Serves:** 4
**40-oz. bowl or 48-oz. pitcher
with blade attachment**

Normally a Mojito is made with rum, lime, mint and sugar cane. Even though passion fruit is referred to as an exotic fruit in the United States, in other countries it is available almost any time of year and is used as an alternative to limes.—Andrea

Shopping List

8 mint leaves

5 ounces passion fruit pulp or ripe pear pulp

⅔ cup light rum

4 cups ice

½ cup passion fruit juice or passion fruit cocktail juice

3 tablespoons sugar

1 Place mint, pulp, rum, ice, juice and sugar into the Ninja 40-oz. bowl with blade in position.

2 Process for 30 to 40 seconds or until completely smooth. Carefully remove blade.

TIP...
Passion fruit pulp and passion fruit cocktail juice can be found in the freezer section of your local supermarket or in Latin grocery stores.

SIPPING SENSATIONS

Frozen Cranberry Cosmopolitan

Prep: 7 min. **Serves:** 4
40-oz. bowl or 48-oz. pitcher with blade attachment

While creating this recipe, we wanted to have a combination of tart and sweetness blended into a frozen drink, which is a nontraditional way to serve a Cosmopolitan. I love serving this drink during the holidays.—Bob

Shopping List

4 cups ice

5 ounces whole fresh cranberries

1 cup cranberry juice

¼ cup triple sec

⅓ cup vodka

4 tablespoons white sugar

1 Place ice, cranberries, juice, triple sec, vodka and sugar into the Ninja 40-oz. bowl with blade in position.

2 Process for 50 to 60 seconds or until completely smooth. Carefully remove blade.

TIP...

If you can't find fresh cranberries because they are not in season, use frozen ones, or use any other fresh fruit like raspberries.

Frozen Sangría

Prep: 12 min. **Serves:** 6
40-oz. bowl or 48-oz. pitcher with blade attachment

Traditionally from Spain, with regional variations, in general sangría is a mix of wine, brandy or cognac, fruit juices, fruit and soda water. You can make it your own by adding any fruit you have. This is a frozen version, typically not served this way, but a novel idea!—Andrea

Shopping List

3 ounces frozen strawberries

3 ounces fresh pineapple, peeled and cored

3 ounces frozen peaches

3 cups ice

½ lime, peeled

½ orange, peeled

1 cup red wine

⅓ cup brandy

1 Place strawberries, pineapple, peaches, ice, lime, orange, wine and brandy into the Ninja 40-oz. bowl with blade in position.

2 Process for 50 to 60 seconds or until drink is completely smooth. Carefully remove blade.

TIP...

Substitute white wine if you prefer instead of the red wine.

Margarita 1 2 3

Prep: 5 min. **Serves:** 3
**40-oz. bowl or 48-oz. pitcher
with blade attachment**

*Traditional margaritas are made
with limes and tequila. This
recipe has a twist, but it can be
used to make any fruit-flavored
margarita you want to create.
Just substitute four ounces of
your favorite fresh fruit for the
lime and orange.—Bob*

Shopping List

4 cups ice

1 cup margarita mix

¼ cup tequila

½ lime, peeled

½ orange, peeled

1 Place ice, margarita mix, tequila, lime
and orange into the Ninja 40-oz. bowl
with blade in position.

2 Process for 40 to 45 seconds or until
completely smooth. Carefully remove
blade.

TIP...
*For a little less
tartness, use lemon
instead of lime.*

Frozen Raspberry Martini

Prep: 5 min. **Serves:** 5
**40-oz. bowl or 48-oz. pitcher
with blade attachment**

*Even if you are not a martini
fan, you may enjoy this flavored
martini. I like them even better
when blended with ice.—Stephen*

Shopping List

4 cups ice

4 ounces whole frozen raspberries

½ cup pomegranate juice

½ cup vodka

¼ cup raspberry liqueur

1 Place ice, raspberries, juice, vodka
and liqueur into the Ninja 40-oz. bowl
with blade in position.

2 Process for 50 to 60 seconds or until
drink is completely smooth. Carefully
remove blade.

TIP...
*You can use frozen
cherries, cherry juice
and cherry liqueur.
Also try frozen peaches,
peach juice and
peach liqueur.*

MOCHA RUSSIAN

Mocha Russian

Prep: 5 min. **Serves:** 4
**40-oz. bowl or 48-oz. pitcher
with blade attachment**

*Chocolate and coffee are two of
the most paired flavors in the
culinary world. This cookbook
had to include this perfect match
that is best served as a drink or
dessert, or in this case, it can be
both a drink and a dessert at the
same time.—Bob*

Shopping List

4 cups ice

⅔ cup vodka

½ cup coffee-flavored liqueur

2 tablespoons chocolate syrup

1 cup half-and-half

1 Place ice, vodka, liqueur, chocolate
syrup and half-and-half into the Ninja
40-oz. bowl with blade in position.

2 Process for 40 to 50 seconds or until
completely smooth. Carefully remove
blade.

TIP...
*Drizzle your glass
with some extra
chocolate syrup to
enhance the flavor.*

Take-Me-Away Piña Colada

Prep: 8 min. **Serves:** 3
**40-oz. bowl or 48-oz. pitcher
with blade attachment**

*This refreshing drink is the
perfect one to have in hand while
admiring a beautiful sunset,
whether you are in Hawaii or in
the comfort of home.—Stephen*

Shopping List

8 ounces fresh pineapple, peeled,
    cored and cut into chunks

4 cups ice

½ cup coconut milk

⅔ cup light rum

1 Place pineapple, ice, coconut milk and
rum into the Ninja 40-oz. bowl with
blade in position.

2 Process for 45 to 55 seconds or until
drink is completely smooth. Carefully
remove blade.

TIP...
*You can use dark
rum instead of the
light rum.*

Frozen Cherry Cuba Libre

Prep: 4 min. **Serves:** 5
40-oz. bowl or 48-oz. pitcher with blade attachment

I love cherry-flavored cola, and whenever I order a Cuba Libre I always ask for it to be added. One night I hosted a guy's poker night and didn't have cherry-flavored cola, but I did have regular cola and some frozen cherries. I got creative and came up with this drink.—Stephen

Shopping List

4 cups ice

3 ounces frozen dark sweet cherries

¾ cup cola-flavored soda

⅔ cup spiced rum

1 lime, peeled and cut in half

1 Place ice, cherries, soda, rum and lime into the Ninja 40-oz. bowl with blade in position.

2 Process for 50 to 60 seconds or until completely smooth. Carefully remove blade.

TIP...

If you love cherry-flavored cola, create a double whammy by using cherry-flavored cola in place of the regular cola.

The Italian Cookie

Prep: 5 min. **Serves:** 3
40-oz. bowl or 48-oz. pitcher with blade attachment

One of the best food memories I have from visiting Florence is having amaretto cookies (Italian macaroons) with a cup of espresso macchiato at a local café. That was the inspiration for creating this drink.—Andrea

Shopping List

4 cups ice

⅓ cup amaretto

¾ cup strong coffee

¼ cup vanilla-flavored liquid coffee creamer

1 Place ice, amaretto, coffee and creamer into the Ninja 40-oz. bowl with blade in position.

2 Process for 40 to 45 seconds or until completely smooth. Carefully remove blade.

TIP...

You can use ¼ cup of half-and-half with 1 teaspoon vanilla and 1½ teaspoons sugar instead of the coffee creamer.

Caribbean Daiquiri

Prep: 6 min. **Serves:** 4
**40-oz. bowl or 48-oz. pitcher
with blade attachment**

The inspiration for this drink came from a trip to Jamaica. While relaxing at the beach, I decided to get a drink at the hotel beach bar that seemed interesting. I came up with my own amazing concoction to share it with you.—Andrea

Shopping List

1 banana, peeled

4 cups ice

⅔ cup grapefruit juice

½ cup coconut-flavored rum

½ lime, peeled and cut in half

1 Place banana, ice, juice, rum and lime into the Ninja 40-oz. bowl with blade in position.

2 Process for 40 to 50 seconds or until completely smooth. Carefully remove blade.

TIP...
This drink also tastes great if you use orange juice instead of grapefruit.

Daiquiri 1 2 3

Prep: 5 min. **Serves:** 3
**40-oz. bowl or 48-oz. pitcher
with blade attachment**

This is a basic recipe with all the right ratios to create any fruit daiquiri drink. Choose your favorite fresh fruit, and pair it with a store-bought daiquiri mix.—Bob

Shopping List

4 cups ice

1 cup daiquiri mix

¼ cup rum

4 ounces fresh fruit

1 Place ice, daiquiri mix, rum and fruit into the Ninja 40-oz. bowl with blade in position.

2 Process for 35 to 45 seconds or until completely smooth. Carefully remove blade.

TIP...
When using fruit with skin, like limes, lemons, oranges, apple, etc., peel the fruit before you use it.

A word from Bob...

Try this great daiquiri with either light or dark rum and you are ready to entertain right at home.

Frozen Blueberry Kamikaze

Prep: 6 min. **Serves:** 4
40-oz. bowl or 48-oz. pitcher with blade attachment

Sometimes you have to fool yourself that you are having a "healthy" alcoholic drink. This drink has three key ingredients that are actually really healthy, full of antioxidants, minerals and vitamins in the fruits it contains.—Stephen

Shopping List

4 cups ice

4 ounces whole frozen blueberries

⅔ cup acai juice

⅔ cup vodka

½ lime, peeled and cut in half

1 Place ice, blueberries, juice, vodka and lime into the Ninja 40-oz. bowl with blade in position.

2 Process for 50 to 60 seconds or until completely smooth. Carefully remove blade.

TIP...

Use any of the different flavor combinations of acai juices on the market: original, blueberry and pomegranate.

White Grape Cosmo Freeze

Prep: 5 min. **Serves:** 3
40-oz. bowl or 48-oz. pitcher with blade attachment

I was having a family picnic in my backyard when this refreshing drink recipe came about. I ran out of my regular juice for Cosmos, and used the kids' white grape juice instead— it was a hit!—Andrea

Shopping List

6 ounces green seedless grapes

4 cups ice

¾ cup white grape juice

⅔ cup vodka

1 Place grapes, ice, juice and vodka into the Ninja 40-oz. bowl with blade in position.

2 Process for 50 to 55 seconds or until completely smooth. Carefully remove blade.

TIP...

You can use red grapes and regular grape juice, if desired.

Purple Potion #6

Prep: 4 min. **Serves:** 1
16-oz. single-serve cup

I recently learned that purple and blue fruits and vegetables contain nutrients like lutein, resveratrol and quercetin. There are so many health benefits to these nutrients that I wanted to create a drink with them.—Stephen

Shopping List

1½ ounces canned or fresh cooked beets

1½ ounces frozen blueberries

1 ounce frozen sweet dark cherries

1 small radish, top and root cut off

⅓ cup acai juice

¼ cup grape juice

1 Place beets, blueberries, cherries, radish and juices into the Ninja 16-oz. cup. Screw on blade cap.

2 Process for 35 to 40 seconds or until completely smooth.

TIP...
Substitute blackberries for the blueberries for a more tart flavor.

Fruit Salad Drink

Prep: 9 min. **Serves:** 1
16-oz. single-serve cup

When I make fruit salad these are the fruits I normally use. One day I didn't have time to sit down and eat, so I decided to blend the fruits and take it to go. It turned out to be equally delicious.—Andrea

Shopping List

¾ ounce peeled, cored, cubed fresh pineapple

1 ounce peeled, pitted, cubed fresh mango

1 ounce green seedless grapes

¼ banana, peeled

1 ounce peeled, cored Granny Smith apple

¼ cup orange juice

1 or 2 ice cubes

1 Place pineapple, mango, grapes, banana, apple, juice and ice in the Ninja 16-oz. cup. Screw on blade cap.

2 Process for 35 to 40 seconds or until completely smooth.

TIP...
For a little extra fiber do not peel the skin of the apple.

Frozen Watermelon Tea

Prep: 5 min. **Freeze:** 6 hours **Serves:** 1
16-oz. single-serve cup

Keep some frozen tea ice cubes in your freezer for this and many other refreshing drinks to keep you cool.—Bob

Shopping List

4 tea ice cubes, made from green or black tea

2 teaspoons honey

2 teaspoons freshly squeezed lemon juice

4 ounces peeled, seeded watermelon cubes

1 Pour brewed tea into ice cube trays and freeze until firm, about 6 hours.

2 Place 4 tea ice cubes, honey, lemon juice and watermelon into the Ninja 16-oz. single-serve cup. Screw on blade cap. Process for 15 seconds or until completely smooth.

3 Serve with fresh mint, if desired.

TIP...
To make frozen tea for more people, it is best to make them individually as written.

Strawberry Tea Frozen Slushie

Prep: 5 min. **Freeze:** 6 hours **Serves:** 1
16-oz. single-serve cup

This refreshment is the easiest to make ever! And it can be made any time of year using frozen, full-flavor strawberries.—Andrea

Shopping List

4 tea ice cubes

6 mint leaves

2 tablespoons confectioners' sugar

½ cup white grape or apple juice

4 ounces frozen strawberries

1 Pour brewed tea into ice cube trays and freeze until firm, about 6 hours.

2 Place mint, sugar and juice into the Ninja 16-oz. single-serve cup. Screw on blade cap. Process for 6 seconds or until well mixed.

3 Add 4 tea ice cubes and the strawberries. Screw on blade cap and process for 6 more seconds or until completely smooth.

TIP...
For a different consistency, adjust the amount of white grape juice—add more if you want more of a drink than a slushie.

Natural Energy

Prep: 10 min. **Serves:** 1
16-oz. single-serve cup

Finding ways to get energy doesn't have to be left to the energy drinks and coffee every morning. This drink is a way you can boost your energy through natural foods without having to worry about any side effects.—Andrea

Shopping List

1 ounce peeled, cored, cubed fresh pineapple

1 ounce frozen blueberries

½ banana, peeled and cut in half

1 kiwi, peeled and cut in half

2 ounces peeled, chopped, seedless watermelon

¼ cup grapefruit juice

⅓ cup unsweetened apple juice

1 Place pineapple, blueberries, banana, kiwi, watermelon and juice into the Ninja 16-oz. cup. Screw on blade cap.

2 Process for 35 to 40 seconds or until completely smooth.

TIP...
For a little extra natural energy, add ½ teaspoon ground flax seeds.

Red Power Punch

Prep: 4 min. **Serves:** 1
16-oz. single-serve cup

We have all heard that the deeper the color of the fruits and vegetables, the more nutritious they are. This deep red fruit drink is full of lycopene, which is known to reduce the risk of cancer.—Bob

Shopping List

1 ounce frozen raspberries

1 ounce frozen strawberries

½ plum tomato, top cut off

½ ounce red leaf greens

¼ cup pomegranate juice

3½ ounces peeled, chopped, seedless watermelon

1 Place raspberries, strawberries, tomato, greens, juice and watermelon into the Ninja 16-oz. cup. Screw on blade cap.

2 Process for 35 to 40 seconds or until completely smooth.

TIP...
Substitute your favorite leafy greens for the red leaf greens.

GOLDEN NECTAR

Golden Nectar

Prep: 8 min. **Serves:** 1
16-oz. single-serve cup

This drink gets its kick from the fresh ginger and the yellow pepper; giving it just a little spicy and salty touch to the really sweet fruits used in this drink.—Stephen

Shopping List

½ ounce yellow bell pepper, seeded

2 ounces peeled, pitted, cubed fresh mango

½ teaspoon minced peeled fresh ginger

½ banana, peeled

2 ounces frozen sliced peaches

⅔ cup passion fruit juice

1 Place pepper, mango, ginger, banana, peaches and juice in the Ninja 16-oz. cup. Screw on blade cap.

2 Process for 35 to 40 seconds or until completely smooth.

TIP...
Substitute mango, peach or apricot nectar for the passion fruit juice for a sweeter drink.

Market Fresh Boost

Prep: 4 min. **Serves:** 1
16-oz. single-serve cup

Even though this drink is full of vegetables, you won't notice that you are drinking an all-veggie concoction. The mango nectar and the ginger help make it really appetizing with a hint of sweetness and touch of spicy.—Bob

Shopping List

1½ ounces fresh, peeled carrots, cut into ½-inch pieces

¼ stalk celery

½ ounce fresh baby spinach

½ plum tomato, top cut off

½ teaspoon minced fresh peeled ginger

1 ounce seeded fresh cucumber (do not peel)

⅓ cup mango nectar

1 or 2 ice cubes

1 Place carrots, celery, spinach, tomato, ginger, cucumber, nectar and ice in the Ninja 16-oz. cup. Screw on blade cap.

2 Process for 35 to 40 seconds or until completely smooth.

TIP...
Add a tablespoon of wheat grass to give it an extra health kick.

Antioxidant Blast

Prep: 4 min. **Serves:** 1
16-oz. single-serve cup

Antioxidants are a great ally when fighting free radicals. Consumed in moderation, antioxidants have been considered beneficial to fight cell damage in our bodies.—Stephen

Shopping List

1 ounce canned or fresh cooked beets

2 ounces frozen strawberries

1½ ounces fresh, peeled carrot, cut into ½-inch pieces

½ ounce fresh baby spinach

½ banana, peeled, cut in half

⅓ cup grapefruit juice

1 Place beets, strawberries, carrot, spinach, banana and juice in the Ninja 16-oz. cup. Screw on blade cap.

2 Process for 35 to 40 seconds or until completely smooth.

TIP...
For an extra anti-oxidant kick, use acai juice instead of the grapefruit juice.

Lean, Mean & Green

Prep: 10 min. **Serves:** 1
16-oz. single-serve cup

Extremely healthy and delicious, this drink has a combination of fruits and vegetables that are loaded with vitamins, minerals and especially chlorophyll, which has been shown to have incredible health benefits.—Bob

Shopping List

1 ounce seeded fresh cucumber (do not peel)

1 ounce green seedless grapes

¼ kiwi, peeled

½ ounce fresh baby spinach

¼ stalk celery

¼ ripe fresh pear, cored (do not peel)

¼ cup white grape juice

1 or 2 ice cubes

1 Place cucumber, grapes, kiwi, spinach, celery, pear, juice and ice in the Ninja 16-oz. cup. Screw on blade cap.

2 Process for 35 to 40 seconds or until completely smooth.

TIP...
For some extra health benefits, add 1 teaspoon spirulina.

DEVILED EGG SALAD   P 46

Sandwiches & Such

Expand your sandwich repertoire with fillings made so quickly in your Ninja! Check out the flavorful twists in Seafood Salad (page 50) and Chicken Salad (page 46).

Then turn to making your own burgers and ground meat concoctions—with only the ingredients you want in them! Burgers go beyond meat, too—look at Vegetarian Black Bean Burger (page 51) for something unique and healthful.

Included in this chapter...

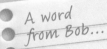

A word from Bob...

Sandwich spreads and fillings can be unique. Cook and chop a couple of slices of cooked bacon or add 2 ounces of chopped cooked ham to most any sandwich for a great taste addition.

Thanks for Turkey Salad

Prep: 6 min. **Serves:** 3
16-oz. chopper bowl with blade attachment

I can't explain how much I love Thanksgiving dishes, especially turkey and cranberry sauce. I always keep a can of cranberry sauce in my pantry, so this sandwich filling was a given.—Stephen

SANDWICHES & SUCH

Shopping List

¼ cup jellied whole cranberry sauce

½ stalk celery, cut into 1-inch pieces

6 ounces cooked turkey breast, cut into 1-inch cubes

2 tablespoons mayonnaise

⅛ teaspoon salt

¾ teaspoon ground black pepper

2 tablespoons French fried onions

1 Place cranberry sauce, celery, turkey, mayonnaise, salt and pepper into the Ninja 16-oz. chopper bowl with blade in position, and pulse 7 times.

2 Carefully remove the blade. Add the French fried onions and mix with a spatula until well mixed.

TIP...
Try this recipe as a sandwich, as a wrap, or serve over salad greens.

Chicken Salad

Prep: 14 min. **Serves:** 4
16-oz. chopper bowl with blade attachment

Tired of the same old chicken salad? Make this Latin inspired version to change it up. Loaded with healthy fats, spices and vegetables, it is a healthier option than your regular chicken salad.—Andrea

Shopping List

1 celery stalk, cut into 1-inch pieces

1 green onion, cut into ½-inch pieces

6 ounces precooked chicken strips

⅓ cup South of the Border Dressing (page 66)

1 Place the celery and onion pieces into the Ninja 16-oz. chopper bowl with blade in position, and pulse 3 to 4 times. Add the chicken strips and pulse 4 to 5 times until coarsely chopped. Carefully remove blade.

2 Stir in the dressing until well mixed.

TIP...
To prepare in the Ninja 40-oz. bowl, multiply the recipe by 3.

Deviled Egg Salad

Prep: 7 min. **Cook:** 7 min. **Serves:** 3
16-oz. chopper bowl with blade attachment

Egg salad with a twist! All the flavors of deviled eggs join the classic egg salad recipe. Eat it for breakfast, lunch, dinner or as a snack with bread or crackers.—Bob

Shopping List

5 hard-cooked eggs, cut in quarters

3 tablespoons mayonnaise

5 sprigs fresh parsley

2 teaspoons Dijon mustard

⅛ teaspoon salt

½ teaspoon ground black pepper

¼ teaspoon Worcestershire sauce

5 dashes hot sauce

½ teaspoon onion powder

1 Place eggs, mayonnaise, parsley, mustard, salt, pepper, Worcestershire sauce, hot sauce and onion powder into the Ninja 16-oz. chopper bowl with blade in position, and pulse 4 times.

2 Remove the lid and carefully scrape down the sides of the bowl with a thin rubber spatula. Replace the lid and pulse 2 more times or until well mixed. Carefully remove blade.

TIP...
To prepare in the Ninja 40-oz. bowl, multiply the recipe by 2.

Ham & Cheese Sandwich

Prep: 8 min. **Cook:** 8 min. **Serves:** 4
16-oz. chopper bowl with blade attachment

This hot sandwich guarantees you'll have a little ham and cheese in every bite. To have it cold, add 1 tablespoon of mayonnaise and 1 teaspoon of red wine vinegar.—Bob

Shopping List

6 ounces cooked ham, cut into cubes

2 ounces provolone cheese, cut into cubes

10 large pitted ripe olives

2 tablespoons mayonnaise

1 tablespoon Italian seasoning

1 teaspoon Dijon mustard

1 teaspoon red wine vinegar

½ teaspoon ground black pepper

8 slices sandwich bread

8 teaspoons unsalted butter

1 Place ham, cheese, olives, mayonnaise, seasoning, mustard, vinegar and pepper into the Ninja 16-oz. chopper bowl with blade in position, and pulse 8 times. Carefully remove blade.

2 Place 4 slices of sandwich bread on a board and divide ham mixture evenly on each slice. Top each with another slice of bread to create a sandwich.

3 Spread 1 teaspoon unsalted butter on one side of each slice of bread.

4 Cook the sandwiches in a large sauté pan over medium heat approximately 4 minutes on each side, or until golden brown and cheese is melted.

TIP...

For a different taste, use pimento-stuffed green olives instead of black olives. Also, use your favorite cheese instead of provolone.

SHRIMP SALAD

Shrimp Salad

Prep: 10 min. **Serves:** 3
16-oz. chopper bowl with blade attachment

This great light summer salad is one of the best. Try it instead of the usual tuna or chicken salad. The secret is using the smoked sausage in the salad.—Bob

Shopping List

3 ounces fully cooked smoked chicken or pork sausage

½ stalk celery, cut into ½-inch cubes

⅛ medium yellow onion, peeled

3 tablespoons mayonnaise

5 sprigs fresh parsley

1 teaspoon Dijon mustard

¼ teaspoon salt

¼ teaspoon ground black pepper

6 ounces cooked, peeled, deveined shrimp

1 tablespoon fresh lemon juice

1 Place sausage, celery, onion, mayonnaise, parsley, mustard, salt, pepper, shrimp and lemon juice into the Ninja 16-oz. chopper bowl with blade in position, and pulse 4 times.

2 Remove the lid and carefully scrape down the sides of the bowl with a thin rubber spatula. Replace the lid and pulse 3 more times until the ingredients are well mixed. Carefully remove blade.

TIP...
Add ½ cup diced fruit to enhance the dish— mango, papaya, pineapple, avocado or watermelon.

Seafood Salad

Prep: 6 min. **Serves:** 3
16-oz. chopper bowl with blade attachment

One of my favorite foods from New England is the lobster roll. Since fresh lobster is not found everywhere and they are quite expensive, try this version that is simple yet delicious.—Stephen

Shopping List

½ stalk celery, cut into ½-inch pieces

⅛ medium yellow onion, peeled

3 tablespoons mayonnaise

¼ cup fresh tarragon

6 ounces imitation crabmeat

4½ teaspoons fresh lemon juice

¼ teaspoon salt

¼ teaspoon ground black pepper

¼ teaspoon Worcestershire sauce

5 dashes lower sodium soy sauce

1 Place celery, onion, mayonnaise, tarragon, crabmeat, lemon juice, salt, pepper, Worcestershire sauce and soy sauce into the Ninja 16-oz. chopper bowl with blade in position, and pulse 4 times.

2 Remove the lid and carefully scrape down the sides of the bowl with a thin rubber spatula. Place the lid back on and pulse 3 more times or until well mixed. Carefully remove blade.

TIP...
Use real crab or lobster pieces instead of the imitation crabmeat. Serve on a hot buttered grilled roll.

Tuna Salad

Prep: 7 min. **Serves:** 4
16-oz. chopper bowl with blade attachment

Everybody knows how to make tuna salad but I like to believe mine is the best. It has the perfect balance of creamy and crunch, salt and spice, tangy and sweet.—Andrea

Shopping List

⅓ cup mayonnaise

⅛ medium yellow onion, peeled

½ celery stalk, cut into 1-inch pieces

3 sprigs fresh parsley

¼ teaspoon salt

½ teaspoon ground black pepper

1 tablespoon plus 1 teaspoon sweet pickle relish

1 tablespoon lemon juice

2 (5-ounce) cans tuna in water, drained

1 Place mayonnaise, onion, celery, parsley, salt, pepper, relish and lemon juice into the Ninja 16-oz. chopper bowl with the blade in position, and pulse 8 times. Carefully remove blade.

2 Place the tuna in a medium mixing bowl. Pour the mayo mixture over the tuna, and stir with a spatula until well mixed.

TIP...
For a healthier tuna salad, substitute nonfat Greek yogurt for the mayonnaise.

Vegetarian Black Bean Burger

Prep: 15 min. **Cook:** 10 min. **Chill:** 1 hour **Serves:** 4
16-oz. chopper bowl with blade attachment

When my "meat-eating" friends come over, they always ask me to cook these burgers. Even though they're made with just beans and vegetables, they have a good meaty texture.—Stephen

Shopping List

1 (15-ounce) can black beans, drained

¼ green bell pepper

⅛ yellow onion, peeled

½ cup baby peeled carrots

½ cup loosely packed cilantro leaves

½ teaspoon garlic powder

¼ teaspoon kosher salt

½ teaspoon ground black pepper

½ teaspoon ground cumin

½ teaspoon ground coriander

1 teaspoon light chili powder

1 teaspoon dried ground oregano

2 tablespoons canned diced green chiles

1 large egg

¾ cup unseasoned bread crumbs

2 teaspoons vegetable oil

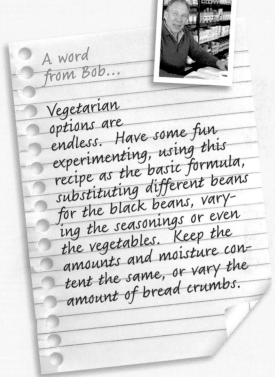

A word from Bob...

Vegetarian options are endless. Have some fun experimenting, using this recipe as the basic formula, substituting different beans for the black beans, varying the seasonings or even the vegetables. Keep the amounts and moisture content the same, or vary the amount of bread crumbs.

1 Set aside ½ cup of the black beans. Place remaining beans, bell pepper, onion, carrots, cilantro, garlic powder, salt, black pepper, cumin, coriander, chili powder, oregano, chiles and egg into the Ninja 16-oz. chopper bowl with blade in position, and pulse 6 times. Process for an additional 10 seconds. Carefully remove blade.

2 Place mixture into a medium-size bowl. Stir in reserved black beans and bread crumbs until well mixed. Form patties and refrigerate for 1 hour.

3 Heat oil in a sauté pan. Add the patties. Cook for 4 to 5 minutes on each side over medium heat or until firm and thoroughly heated.

TIP...
Try adding 2 ounces shredded Cheddar or Pepper Jack cheese to the bean mixture, or substitute red kidney beans for the black beans.

51

Chicken Apple Sausage

Prep: 12 min. **Cook:** 8 min. **Serves:** 6
16-oz. chopper bowl with blade attachment

This sausage variation goes great with eggs or pancakes for breakfast or with pasta and My Alfredo Sauce recipe (page 78), tossed with peppers and onions, or over braised cabbage.—Andrea

Shopping List

3 slices raw bacon, cut into 1-inch pieces

10 ounces boneless skinless chicken thighs, cut into 1-inch cubes

¼ Granny Smith apple, peeled, cored, cut into 3 pieces

⅛ yellow onion, peeled

¼ teaspoon each: dried ground sage, ground ginger and salt

½ teaspoon ground black pepper

⅛ teaspoon ground nutmeg

1 teaspoon maple syrup

1 Place the bacon in the Ninja 16-oz. chopper bowl and process for 6 seconds. Remove and set aside in a mixing bowl.

2 Place the chicken, apple, onion, sage, ginger, salt, black pepper, nutmeg and maple syrup in the 16-oz. chopper bowl with blade in position, and pulse 12 times. Carefully remove blade. Stir in bacon. Form 6 patties.

3 Heat oil in a sauté pan. Add patties. Cook over medium-high heat for 4 minutes on each side.

TIPS...

For a unique side dish, cook this recipe without forming patties. Mix with 10 ounces seasoned stuffing cubes and ¾ cup hot chicken stock.

Meatloaf

Prep: 15 min. **Cook:** 35 min. **Serves:** 4
40-oz. bowl with blade attachment

A classic dish made much faster than with the hand-held meat grinders. You can also use any inexpensive cut of meat.—Andrea

Shopping List

10 ounces boneless lean beef, cubed

⅛ white onion, peeled

2 ounces white bread, cubed

1 large egg

1 ounce whole milk

¾ teaspoon salt

½ teaspoon ground black pepper

½ teaspoon dried thyme

2 cloves garlic, peeled

2 tablespoons ketchup

1 teaspoon Worcestershire sauce

1 Place half the beef cubes in the Ninja 40-oz. bowl with blade in position, then layer the onion, bread, remaining beef, egg, milk, salt, pepper, thyme and garlic; pulse 8 times. Process until well mixed and the mixture pulls away from the sides of the bowl. Carefully remove blade. Form the beef mixture into a loaf shape and place in a baking dish.

2 Mix the ketchup and Worcestershire in a small bowl and brush all over the loaf.

3 Preheat the oven to 375°.

4 Bake for 30 to 40 minutes or until the loaf reaches an internal temperature of 160°. Remove from the oven and let stand for 5 minutes prior to slicing.

Tuna Burger

Prep: 10 min. **Cook:** 6 min. **Serves:** 2
16-oz. chopper bowl with blade attachment

Tuna is a great source of omega-3 fatty acids. Give your family a healthier burger between the bun next time.—Bob

Shopping List

8 ounces fresh tuna

1 green onion, cut into 1-inch pieces

¼ ounce fresh ginger, peeled

1 tablespoon lower sodium soy sauce

½ teaspoon sesame oil

1 teaspoon Dijon mustard

¼ teaspoon ground black pepper

1 tablespoon unseasoned bread crumbs

1 teaspoon vegetable oil

1 Place tuna, onion, ginger, soy sauce, sesame oil, mustard, pepper and bread crumbs into the Ninja 16-oz. chopper bowl with blade in position, and pulse 8 times or until well mixed. Carefully remove blade. Form 2 patties.

2 Heat the oil in a sauté pan. Add patties and cook over medium-high heat for 3 minutes on each side.

TIP...
It is best to cook fresh tuna rare to medium rare so it doesn't become dry.

Turkey Burger

Prep: 14 min. **Cook:** 10 min. **Serves:** 3
16-oz. chopper bowl with blade attachment

One of my vegetarian friends enjoys all the condiments and toppings of a burger, but not the beef. I made these turkey burgers for her and now she is hooked.—Andrea

Shopping List

10 ounces raw turkey breast, cut into 1-inch cubes

2 ounces mozzarella cheese, cut into 1-inch cubes

¼ cup roasted red pepper pieces

1 teaspoon tomato paste

1 tablespoon unseasoned bread crumbs

½ teaspoon garlic powder

½ teaspoon salt

½ teaspoon ground black pepper

½ teaspoon dried basil

1 teaspoon vegetable oil

1 Place turkey, cheese, red pepper, tomato paste, bread crumbs, garlic powder, salt, pepper and basil into the Ninja 16-oz. chopper bowl with blade in position, and pulse 20 times. Carefully remove blade. Form 3 patties.

2 Heat the oil in a sauté pan. Add patties. Cook over medium-high heat for 5 minutes on each side.

TIP...
You can substitute feta cheese for the mozzarella. Serve the cooked burgers with pita bread, sliced cucumber, mint and yogurt.

SANDWICHES & SUCH

Meatballs

Prep: 15 min. **Cook:** 35 min. **Serves:** 12
40-oz. bowl with blade attachment

This is a quick and easy way to make meatballs. Served as an appetizer with a dipping sauce or with pasta and marinara sauce, this is a very versatile recipe.—Bob

Shopping List

10 ounces boneless lean beef, cubed

⅛ white onion, peeled

2 ounces white bread, cubed

2 tablespoons grated Parmesan cheese

¾ teaspoon Italian seasoning

¾ teaspoon salt

¼ teaspoon ground black pepper

1 egg

5 tablespoons milk

1 Place half the beef in the Ninja 40-oz bowl with blade in position. Then place the onion, bread, Parmesan cheese, seasoning, salt, pepper, the remaining beef, egg and milk in the bowl, and pulse 8 times. Process until well mixed and the mixture pulls away from the sides of the bowl. Carefully remove blade.

2 Form mixture into 1-inch meatballs. Place on a baking sheet lined with aluminum foil.

3 Cook at 350° for 30 to 40 minutes or until cooked through.

Sweet Italian Sausage

Prep: 14 min. **Cook:** 10 min. **Serves:** 6
16-oz. chopper bowl with blade attachment

In Italy, you'll find many famous sausages that differ from this type commonly found in the United States. Typically sold as sweet or hot, I love them both.—Stephen

Shopping List

7 slices raw bacon

10 ounces boneless pork loin, cut into 1-inch cubes

¼ teaspoon granulated garlic

¼ teaspoon salt

½ teaspoon ground black pepper

½ teaspoon whole fennel seeds

½ teaspoon sugar

½ teaspoon paprika

1 teaspoon Italian seasoning

3 tablespoons cold water

1 teaspoon vegetable oil

1 Place the bacon in the Ninja 16-oz bowl with the blade in position, and process for 8 seconds. Carefully remove blade. Remove bacon and set aside in a mixing bowl.

2 Place the pork, garlic, salt, pepper, fennel, sugar, paprika, seasoning and water into the Ninja 16-oz. chopper bowl with blade in position, and pulse 20 times or until well mixed. Carefully remove blade. Stir in the bacon and mix well. Form 6 patties, about 2 ounces each.

3 Heat the oil in a sauté pan. Place patties in the pan. Cook over medium-high heat for 5 minutes on each side.

BACON CHEDDAR BURGER

Bacon Cheddar Burger

Prep: 6 min. **Cook:** 10 min. **Serves:** 2
16-oz. chopper bowl with blade attachment

The Bacon Cheddar Cheeseburger is part of the American culture. Unfortunately it has a ton of fat and calories. With this recipe you choose the ingredients that you are putting in your ground beef, making it healthier and tastier.—Stephen

Shopping List

6 ounces boneless lean beef, cut into 1-inch cubes

2 ounces Cheddar cheese, cut into 1-inch cubes

2 slices cooked bacon, cut in 1-inch pieces

¼ teaspoon salt

½ teaspoon ground black pepper

1 teaspoon vegetable oil

1 Layer half of beef cubes, all the cheese, bacon, salt and pepper and the remaining beef cubes into the Ninja 16-oz. bowl with blade in position, and pulse 8 times or until coarsely chopped. Form 2 patties.

2 Heat the oil in a sauté pan. Add patties. Cook over medium-high heat for 5 minutes on each side.

TIPS...

To save some extra calories, use cooked turkey bacon and low-fat cheese.

To double the recipe, use the Ninja 40-oz. bowl.

Sassy Sauces

Our sauces include salad dressings, marinades and rubs, and sauces—everything to enhance the flavor of your standard recipes. The salad dressings offer unique variations recipes—check out Creamy Garlic Dressing (page 63) to use in your next Caesar Salad.

Marinades and rubs are the "before" and sauces are the "after." Use each or both to magnify the taste of your favorite foods. Don't miss the low-fat My Alfredo Sauce (page 78) recipe. Your next pasta dish will get raves.

A word from Bob...

Using your Ninja blender allows you to create fabulous sauces in mere minutes. Homemade, fast, and delicious!

Included in this chapter...

Creamy Garlic Dressing

Prep: 10 min. **Yield:** 1¼ cups
16-oz. chopper bowl with blade attachment

This recipe re-creates the flavors of a Caesar dressing without the anchovies. To make it easier, the Parmesan is already in it so you don't have to grate any on top. Try it during the summer with grilled Romaine lettuce.—Andrea

Shopping List

1 cup plus 2 tablespoons mayonnaise

5 cloves garlic, peeled

2 tablespoons freshly squeezed lemon juice

¼ cup red wine vinegar

1 wedge Parmesan cheese (1½ ounces), cut into ½-inch pieces

½ teaspoon ground black pepper

1 Place mayonnaise, garlic, lemon juice, vinegar, cheese and pepper in the Ninja 16-oz. chopper bowl with blade in position.

2 Process for 20 seconds or until well mixed. Carefully remove blade.

3 Refrigerate.

TIP...
For a sweeter and less pungent flavor, roast the garlic with 1 teaspoon extra virgin olive oil for 15 minutes at 350° in the oven.

Herb and Mustard Vinaigrette

Prep: 5 min. **Yield:** 1½ cups
16-oz. chopper bowl with blade attachment

This is a traditional salad dressing, used widely in France, that pairs well with any salad.—Andrea

Shopping List

1 cup olive oil

⅓ cup white wine vinegar

½ teaspoon salt

¼ teaspoon white pepper

1 tablespoon Dijon mustard

1 small clove garlic, peeled

5 sprigs Italian flat leaf parsley

¼ shallot, peeled

1 Place oil, vinegar, salt, pepper, mustard, garlic, parsley and shallot in the Ninja 16-oz. chopper bowl with blade in position.

2 Process until thickened and well mixed. Carefully remove blade.

3 Refrigerate.

TIP...
Substitute any vinegar of your choice for the white wine vinegar, and red onion for the shallot.

Italian Vinaigrette

Prep: 10 min. **Yield:** 1½ cups
16-oz. chopper bowl with blade attachment

Although this vinaigrette is uncommon in Italy, you'll always find some version in many American refrigerators. You can add many of your favorite ingredients to make this vinaigrette different each time.—Bob

Shopping List

2 cloves garlic, peeled

½ yellow onion, peeled, cut into thirds

¼ red bell pepper, cored, cut into 4 pieces

¾ cup extra virgin olive oil

⅓ cup red wine vinegar

1 teaspoon Italian seasoning

½ teaspoon sugar

½ teaspoon salt

¼ teaspoon ground black pepper

1 Place garlic, onion, bell pepper, oil, vinegar, seasoning, sugar, salt and black pepper in the Ninja 16-oz. chopper bowl with blade in position.

2 Process for 10 seconds or until well mixed. Carefully remove blade.

3 Refrigerate.

TIP...

For a fresher version, use ¼ cup loosely packed basil, oregano and parsley instead of the Italian seasoning.

Balsamic Vinaigrette

Prep: 5 min. **Yield:** 1½ cups
16-oz. chopper bowl with blade attachment

Balsamic vinegar is the jewel of all vinegars. Its complexity in flavor from sour, sweet and woodsy results in an intense, mouthwatering pleasure. This recipe enhances all those characteristics without overpowering any other.—Stephen

Shopping List

¾ cup extra virgin olive oil

⅓ cup balsamic vinegar

2 cloves garlic, peeled

2 teaspoons Dijon mustard

½ teaspoon dried oregano

½ teaspoon dried basil

½ teaspoon sugar

½ teaspoon salt

¼ teaspoon ground black pepper

1 Place oil, vinegar, garlic, mustard, oregano, basil, sugar, salt and pepper in the Ninja 16-oz. chopper bowl with blade in position.

2 Process for 10 seconds or until well mixed. Carefully remove blade.

3 Refrigerate.

TIP...

For another wonderful taste, try white balsamic vinegar. This vinaigrette will keep in your refrigerator up to a month. Use with any salad, as a dip for bread, or tossed with fresh tomatoes.

Dill Dressing

Prep: 10 min. **Yield:** 1¼ cups
16-oz. chopper bowl with blade attachment

Traditionally, cold potato salad is not served with dill. My neighbor had a potato salad with dill dressing and I could not stop eating it. I created this recipe and haven't made the classic version again.—Andrea

Shopping List

1 cup mayonnaise

¾ cup sour cream

1 cup fresh dill, tightly packed

2 teaspoons Dijon mustard

1 clove garlic, peeled

⅓ cup apple cider vinegar

1 teaspoon kosher salt

1 teaspoon ground black pepper

1 Place mayonnaise, sour cream, dill, mustard, garlic, vinegar, salt and pepper in the Ninja 16-oz. chopper bowl with blade in position.

2 Process for 20 seconds or until well mixed. Carefully remove blade.

3 Refrigerate.

TIP...

Use this dressing for your next cucumber salad. Also spread it on grilled salmon, or as a dip for crudité.

French Dressing

Prep: 7 min. **Yield:** 1½ cups
16-oz. chopper bowl with blade attachment

The commercial American dressing that is creamy, tartly sweet and red-orange in color is one you will never find in Europe. I prefer to make it at home.—Andrea

Shopping List

¾ cup vegetable oil

⅓ cup white vinegar

3 tablespoons ketchup

½ teaspoon Worcestershire sauce

½ teaspoon dry mustard

1 teaspoon sugar

½ teaspoon salt

¼ teaspoon ground black pepper

1 Place oil, vinegar, ketchup, Worcestershire sauce, mustard, sugar, salt and pepper in the Ninja 16-oz. chopper bowl with blade in position.

2 Process for 15 seconds or until well mixed. Carefully remove blade.

3 Refrigerate.

Bacon Dressing

Prep: 20 min. **Yield:** 1¾ cups
16-oz. chopper bowl with blade attachment

I am a big fan of German potato salad, which is served with a warm bacon dressing. I wanted to create a version of this classic that can be served either hot or cold.—Andrea

Shopping List

4 slices cooked bacon, cut into 1-inch pieces

½ cup cilantro, washed, trimmed

½ cup vegetable oil

¼ cup extra virgin olive oil

⅓ cup apple cider vinegar

1 tablespoon Dijon mustard

1½ teaspoons ground ginger

½ teaspoon ground black pepper

¼ teaspoon kosher salt

½ cup sour cream

1 Place bacon, cilantro, oils, vinegar, mustard, ginger, pepper, salt and sour cream in the Ninja 16-oz. chopper bowl with blade in position.

2 Process for 20 seconds or until well mixed. Carefully remove blade.

3 Refrigerate.

4 To serve warm, pour into a medium saucepan. Heat on low until warmed.

TIP...
Most often served with spinach salad, try this dressing atop cooked vegetables or as a dip with some crusty bread.

South of the Border Dressing

Prep: 10 min. **Yield:** 1¾ cups
16-oz. chopper bowl with blade attachment

If you're in the mood for Mexican food, but don't want all the calories, fat and carbs, fill your plate with fresh greens and vegetables, then use this dressing with the spices and flavors from south of the border.—Stephen

Shopping List

1 tablespoon canned chopped green chiles

1 teaspoon chopped chipotle pepper in adobo sauce

1 lime, peeled, cut in half

1 avocado, peeled, seeded, and cut in quarters

½ cup cilantro, washed, trimmed

½ cup cold water

2 tablespoons white vinegar

1 cup nonfat Greek yogurt

1 tablespoon light chili powder

1 teaspoon ground cumin

1 teaspoon ground coriander

½ teaspoon kosher salt

½ teaspoon ground black pepper

1 Place chiles, chipotle pepper, lime, avocado, cilantro, water, vinegar, yogurt, chili powder, cumin, coriander, salt and pepper in the Ninja 16-oz. chopper bowl with blade in position.

2 Process for 10 seconds or until well mixed. Carefully remove blade.

3 Refrigerate.

Thousand Island Dressing

Prep: 10 min. **Yield:** 1½ cups
16-oz. chopper bowl with blade attachment

The classic Reuben sandwich needs to have an outstanding dressing to be spread right on the rye bread. After you make this dressing, you'll see what we mean.—Bob

Shopping List

1 cup mayonnaise

¼ yellow onion, cut in half

12 pimento-stuffed green olives

¼ cup white vinegar

¼ cup chili sauce

2 tablespoons dill pickle relish

1 teaspoon Worcestershire sauce

½ teaspoon sugar

¼ teaspoon ground black pepper

2 dashes hot sauce

1 Place mayonnaise, onion, olives, vinegar, chili sauce, relish, Worcestershire sauce, sugar, pepper, and hot sauce in the Ninja 16-oz. chopper bowl with blade in position.

2 Process for 15 seconds or until well mixed. Carefully remove blade.

3 Refrigerate.

Miso Vinaigrette

Prep: 10 min. **Yield:** 1½ cups
16-oz. chopper bowl with blade attachment

Miso is a traditional Japanese seasoning produced by fermenting soy beans with salt. Most commonly used in soups, it is actually a complement to the flavor in this vinaigrette. I like it with shredded cabbage, greens or even a fresh tuna steak.—Stephen

Shopping List

¼ shallot, peeled

2 tablespoons minced pickled ginger

1 green onion, cut into 1-inch pieces

3 tablespoons white miso paste

¼ cup lower sodium soy sauce

⅓ cup rice wine vinegar

1 tablespoon sesame oil

1 tablespoon Dijon mustard

1 tablespoon honey

¾ cup vegetable oil

½ teaspoon ground black pepper

1 Place shallot, ginger, green onion, miso paste, soy sauce, vinegar, sesame oil, mustard, honey, vegetable oil and black pepper in the Ninja 16-oz. chopper bowl with blade in position.

2 Process for 20 seconds or until well mixed. Carefully remove blade.

3 Refrigerate.

TIP...

Miso is sold in Asian markets or specialty supermarkets.

Adobo Marinade

Prep: 10 min. **Yield:** 12 ounces
16-oz. chopper bowl with blade attachment

Adobo is a traditional marinade used in Latin America where spices vary from one country to the next. As with all marinades, this recipe enhances the flavor greatly.—Bob

Shopping List

¾ cup red wine vinegar

4 ounces vegetable oil

2 tablespoons dried oregano

3 tablespoons ground cumin

2 tablespoons paprika

1½ teaspoons salt

1½ teaspoons ground black pepper

1½ ounces dried chiles

6 cloves garlic, peeled

¾ cup cold water

1 Place vinegar, oil, oregano, cumin, paprika, salt, pepper, chiles, garlic and water in the Ninja 16-oz. chopper bowl with blade in position.

2 Process for 15 to 20 seconds. Carefully remove blade.

3 Cover and refrigerate.

TIP...

Marinate 2 pounds of pork loin chops for 24 hours. Grill or pan-sauté for 8 minutes on each side over medium heat. Serve with Sweet Plantain Mash (page 131).

Asian Marinade

Prep: 15 min. **Yield:** 14 ounces
16-oz. chopper bowl with blade attachment

The versatility and depth of flavor in this recipe lends itself to as many ideas as you can consider.—Stephen

Shopping List

2 cloves garlic, peeled

½ ounce peeled fresh ginger

½ medium shallot, peeled

2 fresh serrano chiles, top cut off and cut in half

1 tablespoon sugar

1 whole lime, peeled, cut in half

2 tablespoons rice wine vinegar

½ cup lower sodium soy sauce

1 green onion, cut into 1-inch pieces

1 whole pear, peeled, cored, cut into chunks

¼ cup cold water

½ teaspoon ground black pepper

1 Place all ingredients in the Ninja 16-oz. chopper bowl with blade in position.

2 Process for 30 seconds. Carefully remove blade.

3 Place the marinade into a sealed container and refrigerate up to 1 week.

TIP...

Marinate 2 pounds of sliced New York strip steak, chicken or pork. Pan-sauté and serve over rice and vegetables.

Yogurt Marinade

Prep: 12 min. **Yield:** 16 ounces
16-oz. chopper bowl with blade attachment

Yogurt is a natural tenderizer and will produce a flavorful, golden crust with the combination of these ingredients. It only takes a few hours for all the flavors to be absorbed.—Stephen

Shopping List

1 cup low-fat Greek yogurt

2 cloves garlic, peeled

½ cup mint leaves, loosely packed

¼ cup extra virgin olive oil

¼ cup red wine vinegar

1 tablespoon freshly squeezed lemon juice

½ teaspoon ground black pepper

¼ teaspoon salt

¼ cup Garam Masala Rub (page 73)

1 Place yogurt, garlic, mint, olive oil, vinegar, lemon juice, pepper and salt in the Ninja 16-oz. chopper bowl with blade in position, and process for 20 seconds. Carefully remove blade.

2 Pour the mixture into a mixing bowl, and stir in the Garam Masala Rub.

3 Place the marinade into a sealed container, and refrigerate up to 1 week.

SASSY SAUCES

TIP...

No need to wait overnight for this marinade—3 hours will do it.

Mediterranean Marinade

Prep: 10 min. **Yield:** 12 ounces
16-oz. chopper bowl with blade attachment

These are my fondest ingredients and take me back to a time similar to the history and culture in which I grew up. The smells and tastes are like old friends each time they meet.—Andrea

Shopping List

2 cloves garlic, peeled

2 teaspoons dried thyme

2 teaspoons dried oregano

2 teaspoons dried basil

1 teaspoon ground black pepper

½ teaspoon salt

¾ cup extra virgin olive oil

¼ cup orange juice

1½ teaspoons fennel seed

¼ cup sherry vinegar

1 Place garlic, thyme, oregano, basil, pepper, salt, olive oil, orange juice, fennel and vinegar in the Ninja 16-oz. chopper bowl with blade in position, and process for 15 to 20 seconds or until well mixed. Carefully remove blade.

2 Place the marinade into a sealed container, and refrigerate up to 1 week.

TIP...
Pour this marinade atop 2 pounds of chicken, pork or lamb in a container and marinate for 24 hours. For fish, marinate for 8 hours.

Fajita Marinade

Prep: 12 min. **Yield:** 12 ounces
16-oz. chopper bowl with blade attachment

Here's a recipe that is so simple to make. After it is cooked, you'll find the flavor and smell that touches your memory of your favorite Mexican restaurant. Now, all you need is a good margarita.—Bob

Shopping List

2 cloves garlic, peeled

2 teaspoons dried oregano

⅛ medium yellow onion

1 tablespoon ground cumin

3 dried chiles

1 teaspoon Worcestershire sauce

½ cup fresh cilantro leaves

2 limes, peeled and cut in half

½ cup cold water

1 teaspoon ground black pepper

¼ cup lower sodium soy sauce

1 tablespoon honey

1 Place garlic, oregano, onion, cumin, chiles, Worcestershire sauce, cilantro, limes, water, pepper, soy sauce and honey in the Ninja 16-oz. chopper bowl with blade in position, and process for 20 to 25 seconds or until well mixed. Carefully remove blade.

2 Cover and refrigerate.

TIP...

Marinate 2 pounds of your favorite sliced meat for 24 hours. Sauté for 5 minutes over medium-high heat. Serve with warm flour tortillas, sour cream, guacamole, sautéed peppers and onions, cheese and tomato.

Grapefruit Mojo

Prep: 13 min. **Yield:** 14 ounces
16-oz. chopper bowl with blade attachment

Mojo is a very popular condiment used throughout the Caribbean islands as a sauce, marinade or dip. Grapefruit tasted the best because it had a little more sweetness than the others.—Stephen

Shopping List

¼ cup extra virgin olive oil

2 cloves garlic, peeled

1 whole medium shallot, peeled, cut in half

¾ teaspoon salt

¾ teaspoon ground black pepper

1 teaspoon dried oregano

1½ teaspoons ground cumin

¼ cup fresh cilantro leaves

1 whole grapefruit, peeled, seeded and cut
  in fourths

1 whole lime, peeled, cut in half

1 Place olive oil, garlic, shallot, salt, pepper, oregano, cumin, cilantro, grapefruit and lime in the Ninja 16-oz. chopper bowl with blade in position, and process for 30 seconds. Carefully remove blade.

2 Place the marinade into a sealed container and refrigerate up to 1 week.

TIP...
Marinate 2 pounds chicken breasts with 1 sliced onion and the mojo for 24 hours. Sauté chicken breasts. Add the mojo and onions, and cook until chicken is cooked and onions are soft.

Garam Masala Rub

Prep: 20 min. **Cook:** 5 min. **Yield:** 1 cup
16-oz. chopper bowl with blade attachment

Garam Masala is a common North Indian pungent spice blend. Toasting the spices brings out their flavor and aromas.—Andrea

Shopping List

4 tablespoons black peppercorns

1 teaspoon whole cloves

2 tablespoons coriander seeds

2 tablespoons cumin seeds

2 tablespoons mustard seeds

2 tablespoons fennel seeds

2 teaspoons onion powder

1 teaspoon ground cinnamon

½ ounce dried chiles

¼ cup ground turmeric

1 Toast peppercorns and cloves, coriander, cumin, mustard and fennel seeds together in a sauté pan over medium heat for 5 minutes. Set aside and let cool completely.

2 Place toasted mixture, onion powder, cinnamon and chiles in the Ninja 16-oz. chopper bowl with blade in position, and process for 1 minute. Carefully remove blade. Stir in the turmeric until well mixed.

3 Place the mixture into a sealed bag or container and store up to 6 months or until flavors start to fade.

TIP...

Use as a dry rub for meats, or add it to vegetables, stews and salad dressings.

Cajun Olive Oil Rub

Prep: 10 min. **Yield:** about ¾ cup
16-oz. single-serve cup

Some of your favorite flavors add so much with even a short time of marinating, but several hours is best if you can spare the time.—Bob

Shopping List

2 cloves garlic, peeled

½ cup packed fresh parsley leaves

¼ cup freshly squeezed lemon juice

2 teaspoons lemon zest

2 teaspoons honey mustard

3 tablespoons Cajun seasoning

½ cup olive oil

1 Place garlic, parsley, lemon juice and zest, honey mustard, seasonings and olive oil into the single-serve cup. Screw on blade cap.

2 Process for 5 seconds or until well mixed. Refrigerate until ready to use, up to 1 month.

TIP...

This rub is especially delicious with shrimp. Pour half the rub into a zipper-top bag with 1 pound of peeled, deveined large shrimp and shake to coat. Marinate 1 hour or overnight, then cook as desired.

Jerk Rub

Prep: 16 min. **Yield:** 12 ounces
16-oz. chopper bowl with blade attachment

After using this wet rub on your favorite dish, you'll feel like you're at one of those local fast food Jamaican jerk shacks.—Bob

Shopping List

3 green onions, cut into 1-inch pieces

2 habanero peppers, stems cut off, cut in half

½ teaspoon ground black pepper

½ cup vegetable oil

2 teaspoons ground allspice

3 tablespoons freshly squeezed lemon juice

2 tablespoons light brown sugar

1½ teaspoons dried thyme

3 cloves garlic, peeled

¾ ounce fresh ginger, peeled

¼ medium yellow onion

1 tablespoon lower sodium soy sauce

1 tablespoon Worcestershire sauce

2 tablespoons white vinegar

1 Place green onions, peppers, black pepper, oil, allspice, lemon juice, brown sugar, thyme, garlic, ginger, onion, soy sauce, Worcestershire sauce and vinegar in the Ninja 16-oz. chopper bowl with blade in position, and process for 30 seconds. Carefully remove blade.

2 Place the rub into a sealed container, and refrigerate up to 1 week.

TIP...
Jerk refers to both a cooking method and a seasoning.

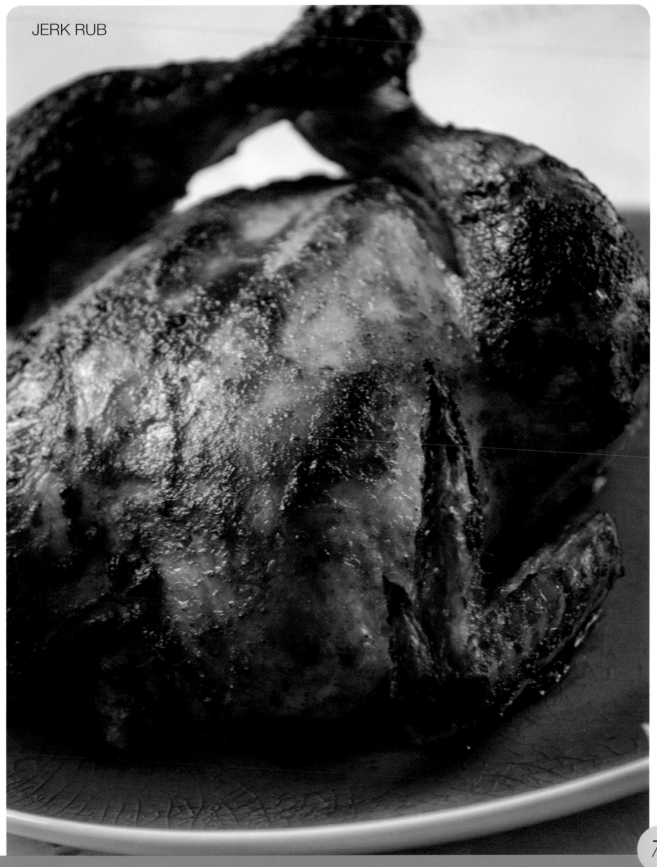

JERK RUB

SUN-DRIED TOMATO PESTO

Sun-Dried Tomato Pesto

Prep: 10 min. **Yield:** 1¼ cups
16-oz. chopper bowl with blade attachment

Most of the time I make a marinara sauce for the pasta I love, but to change it up a little, I try to come up with different pesto recipes. One of my all-time favorite ingredients is sun-dried tomatoes.—Andrea

Shopping List

1 cup sun-dried tomatoes, packed in oil

12 large leaves fresh basil

¼ cup fresh parsley leaves

2 cloves garlic, peeled

2 tablespoons balsamic vinegar

1 ounce grated Parmesan cheese

⅓ cup extra virgin olive oil

½ teaspoon salt

½ teaspoon ground black pepper

⅓ cup walnuts, toasted

1 Place sun-dried tomatoes, basil, parsley, garlic, vinegar, cheese, olive oil, salt, pepper, and walnuts in the Ninja 16-oz. chopper bowl with blade in position.

2 Process until sauce is smooth and well mixed. Carefully remove blade.

3 Refrigerate.

TIP...
Add 1 cup heavy cream to create a creamy sauce for your favorite pasta.

Steak Sauce

Prep: 10 min. **Cook:** 15 min.
Cool: 15 min. **Yield:** 1½ cups
16-oz. chopper bowl with blade attachment

This steak sauce is well balanced and unique, especially when compared to the steak sauce you find in the market.—Bob

Shopping List

4 tablespoons unsalted butter

1 ounce Worcestershire sauce

1 tablespoon hot pepper sauce

1 tablespoon freshly squeezed lemon juice

2 cloves garlic, peeled

2 tablespoons Dijon mustard

¼ cup dark raisins

2 ounces orange juice

¼ cup ketchup

½ cup vegetable stock

½ teaspoon each: salt and black pepper

1 Add all ingredients into a medium saucepan. Bring to a boil then reduce heat to medium.

2 Cook 15 minutes, stirring occasionally. Remove from heat; let cool 15 minutes.

3 Place the mixture in the Ninja 16-oz. chopper bowl with blade in position, and process until sauce is smooth and well mixed. Carefully remove blade.

4 Refrigerate.

TIP...
For a special touch, substitute red wine for the orange juice, and add a pinch of ground cloves and ½ teaspoon of dried thyme.

Pizza Sauce

Prep: 18 min. **Chill:** 15 min. **Yield:** 1½ cups
16-oz. single-serve cup or chopper bowl

This basic pizza sauce recipe is the best, with a lot of flavor . . . and really easy to make. Make it fresh every time you make a pizza. If you like it a little spicy, add ¼ teaspoon of red pepper flakes.—Bob

Shopping List

1 (7-ounce) can whole peeled tomatoes, drained

1 small clove garlic, peeled

⅛ medium white onion, peeled

¼ teaspoon salt

⅛ teaspoon black pepper

⅛ teaspoon Italian seasoning

3 fresh basil leaves

1 Place tomatoes, garlic, onion, salt, pepper, Italian seasoning and basil in the Ninja 16-oz cup.

2 Process until sauce is smooth and well mixed.

3 Refrigerate for 15 minutes.

4 Spread on Whole-Wheat Pizza Dough (page 108)

TIP...

Add fresh oregano and parsley to create different variations.

If tripling the recipe, use the 40-oz. bowl.

My Alfredo Sauce

Prep: 6 min. **Cook:** 5 min. **Yield:** About 1 quart
40-oz. bowl with blade attachment

Delicious creamy pasta Alfredo is one of my favorite Italian pasta dishes, but it is packed with fat calories, is really heavy and takes a while to make. This recipe has the same great flavor, but with a lot fewer calories.—Andrea

Shopping List

1 (8-ounce) package reduced-fat cream cheese

4½ ounces Parmesan cheese, cut into ½-inch pieces

1½ cups reduced-fat (2%) milk

1½ teaspoons ground black pepper

Pasta, your choice, cooked and drained

1 Place cream cheese, Parmesan cheese, milk, and pepper in the Ninja 40-oz. bowl with blade in position.

2 Process until sauce is smooth and well mixed. There will be some small crumb size pieces of Parmesan cheese. Carefully remove blade.

3 Pour sauce into a medium saucepan with warm pasta.

4 Heat 5 minutes or until sauce is hot, stirring occasionally.

TIP...

You can substitute skim milk for 2% milk to save extra calories.

Basic Marinara Sauce

Prep: 8 min. **Cook:** 30 min. **Yield:** About 1 quart
40-oz. bowl with blade attachment

This really quick and easy versatile recipe can be used for lasagna, chicken or eggplant Parmesan, meatballs, as a dipping sauce, or just plain spaghetti.—Stephen

Shopping List

1 (28-ounce) can whole peeled tomatoes, undrained

2 vine ripe tomatoes, top cut off and quartered

4 cloves garlic, peeled

½ white onion, peeled

1¼ cups chicken stock

1 teaspoon salt

½ teaspoon black pepper

6 fresh basil leaves

2 sprigs flat leaf parsley

1 Place canned tomatoes, fresh tomatoes, garlic, onion, chicken stock, salt, pepper, basil and parsley into the Ninja 40-oz. bowl with blade in position.

2 Process until sauce is smooth and well mixed. Carefully remove blade.

3 Pour sauce into a medium saucepan.

4 Cook over low heat for 30 to 40 minutes or until hot, stirring occasionally.

TIP...
Store in the freezer up to a month.

Hot and Sour Sauce

Prep: 10 min. **Cook:** 25 min. **Yield:** 3 cups
40-oz. bowl with blade attachment

This low-calorie Asian-inspired sauce is easy to make and tastes wonderful with so many foods. It can be used as a sauce or a dipping sauce. My favorite pairing is tempura shrimp served with steamed rice and vegetables.—Stephen

Shopping List

1 tablespoon sesame oil

1 (20-ounce) can crushed pineapple

⅓ cup ketchup

¼ cup rice wine vinegar

¼ cup lower sodium soy sauce

2 serrano chiles, seeds removed

2 green onions

1 clove garlic, peeled

¼ ounce fresh ginger, peeled

½ cup water

1 Place oil, pineapple and juice, ketchup, vinegar, soy sauce, chiles, onions, garlic, ginger and water in the Ninja 40-oz. bowl with blade in position.

2 Process until sauce is smooth and well mixed. Carefully remove blade.

3 Pour the mixture in a medium saucepan. Bring to a boil, then reduce heat to medium.

4 Cook 20 minutes, or until hot and slightly thickened, stirring occasionally.

5 Refrigerate.

TIP...
Substitute apricot preserves for the crushed pineapple for a flavor change.

Chinese Barbeque Sauce

Prep: 6 min. **Yield:** 1 cup
16-oz. chopper bowl with blade attachment

Whether it is ribs or chicken wings, whatever you glaze with this non-ketchup-based barbeque sauce will be finger-licking good. For my vegetarian friends, I brush this on tofu prior to grilling to give it a crispy texture on the outside.—Andrea

Shopping List

2 cloves garlic, peeled

½ ounce fresh ginger, peeled

4 ounces hoisin sauce

¼ cup sherry wine

¼ cup lower sodium soy sauce

⅛ teaspoon five spice powder

1 teaspoon light brown sugar

1 Place garlic, ginger, hoisin sauce, sherry, soy sauce, five spice powder and brown sugar in the Ninja 16-oz. chopper bowl, and process until the sauce is smooth and well mixed. Carefully remove blade.

2 Refrigerate.

TIP...
For grilling, brush sauce on shrimp, tuna, pork chops or vegetables just before serving.

Spicy Peanut Sauce

Prep: 10 min. **Yield:** 1½ cups
16-oz. chopper bowl with blade attachment

*Instead of going out to lunch one day, I whipped up something healthy from my refrigerator. Enjoy this sauce as a dip, mixed with noodles or tossed with greens.
—Andrea*

Shopping List

½ teaspoon garlic powder

2 tablespoons pickled ginger

1 tablespoon sesame oil

¼ cup lower sodium soy sauce

½ cup creamy peanut butter

¼ cup orange juice

1 tablespoon light brown sugar

2 tablespoons sambal

2 tablespoons hoisin sauce

1 Place garlic powder, ginger, oil, soy sauce, peanut butter, orange juice, brown sugar, sambal, and hoisin sauce in the Ninja 16-oz. chopper bowl with blade in position.

2 Process for 20 seconds or until puréed. Carefully remove blade.

3 Refrigerate.

TIP...
Sambal is a chile-based Southeast Asian condiment.

Giardiniera Aïoli

Prep: 10 min. **Yield:** 2 cups
16-oz. chopper bowl with blade attachment

Giardiniera is a relish of assorted pickled vegetables, typically cauliflower, carrots, celery and peppers covered in vinegar and found in the condiment section of most markets. This version is a twist on another favorite for fish—tartar sauce.—Bob

Shopping List

1 cup giardiniera

¾ cup mayonnaise

2 teaspoons Dijon mustard

2 tablespoons freshly squeezed lemon juice

¼ cup fresh parsley leaves

¼ teaspoon ground black pepper

2 dill pickle spears

1 Place giardiniera, mayonnaise, mustard, lemon juice, parsley, pepper and pickles in the Ninja 16-oz. chopper bowl.

2 Process until sauce is smooth and well mixed. Carefully remove blade.

3 Refrigerate.

TIP...
For a little spice, add 1 whole jalapeño, top sliced off, while processing. For some crunch, process only 10 to 15 seconds.

Roasted Red Pepper Aïoli

Prep: 10 min. **Cook:** 15 min. **Yield:** 1¾ cups
16-oz. chopper bowl with blade attachment

Aïoli, also known as garlic mayonnaise, has many uses, such as a sandwich spread, vegetable or French fry dip, sauce for seafood or meat, and as a table condiment for bread.—Bob

Shopping List

1 cup roasted red peppers

2 cloves garlic, peeled

¾ cup mayonnaise

1 tablespoon freshly squeezed lemon juice

1 tablespoon capers

8 large leaves fresh basil

¼ cup fresh parsley leaves

½ teaspoon ground black pepper

¼ teaspoon salt

1 Place roasted peppers, garlic, mayonnaise, lemon juice, capers, basil, parsley, pepper and salt in the Ninja 16-oz. chopper bowl with blade in position.

2 Process until sauce is smooth and well mixed. Carefully remove blade.

3 Refrigerate.

TIP...
Substitute cooked eggplant, canned artichokes or avocado for the roasted red peppers.

ALMOND WAFFLE   P 91

Breakfast & The Bakery

There is nothing like the Ninja to help get breakfast on the table. Mix all kinds of batter—pancakes, muffins, scones and waffles—ready in a flash. For an international flair, make South American Corn Pancakes (page 93) soon.

Enter the bakery right in your own kitchen—biscuits, bread, pastry doughs and cookies you can make after school with your family! Enjoy the anytime Spice-Me-Up Cookies (page 99). Don't wait for the holidays.

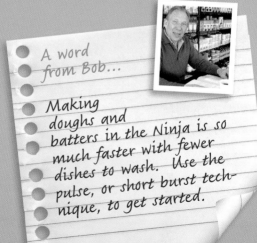

A word from Bob...

Making doughs and batters in the Ninja is so much faster with fewer dishes to wash. Use the pulse, or short burst technique, to get started.

Included in this chapter...

Apple Muffins

Prep: 20 min. **Cook:** 30 min. **Serves:** 12
40-oz. bowl with blade attachment

Kids love these muffins as a snack or for breakfast and the best part is that they are eating fruit and fiber without even knowing it.—Stephen

Shopping List

1 Golden Delicious apple, peeled, cored and quartered

1 Granny Smith apple, peeled, cored and quartered

1½ cups wheat germ

1 cup all-purpose flour

1 teaspoon baking soda

1 teaspoon baking powder

1 teaspoon salt

2 teaspoons ground cinnamon

1 cup buttermilk

⅓ cup vegetable oil

⅔ cup light brown sugar

1 egg

1 teaspoon vanilla extract

¼ cup sugar crystals

TIP...

Use 2 pears instead of 2 apples for a different take on this recipe.

1 Preheat oven to 350°. Line a 12-cup muffin pan with paper cupcake liners.

2 Place quartered apples into the Ninja 40-oz. bowl with blade in position, and pulse 8 times or until coarsely chopped. Carefully remove blade. Place apples into a colander.

3 Whisk wheat germ, flour, baking soda, baking powder, salt and cinnamon in a mixing bowl and whisk until well mixed.

4 Pour the buttermilk, oil and brown sugar into the same Ninja bowl with blade in position. Add the flour mixture, egg and vanilla and process for 10 to 15 seconds or until well mixed. Carefully remove blade, add the apples and fold them with a spatula until well mixed. Spoon mixture into prepared muffin pan, filling about ¾ full. Sprinkle sugar crystals equally on top.

5 Bake for 25 to 30 minutes or until a wooden pick inserted in the middle comes out clean. Cool on a cooling rack.

BREAKFAST & THE BAKERY

Strawberry Muffins

Prep: 25 min. **Cook:** 40 min. **Serves:** 12
40-oz. bowl with blade attachment

These are my favorite muffins to have for breakfast. They are sweet but tangy, moist but not oily. If berries are not in season, use frozen ones that are completely thawed and drained before processing.—Stephen

Shopping List

1 quart fresh strawberries, top stems cut off

1 teaspoon fresh lemon juice

¼ cup vegetable oil

½ cup milk

¼ cup sour cream

1 cup sugar

2 cups all-purpose flour

2 teaspoons baking powder

½ teaspoon salt

1 teaspoon vanilla extract

1 egg

1 Preheat oven to 350°. Line a 12-cup muffin pan with paper cupcake liners.

2 Place strawberries and lemon juice into the Ninja 40-oz. bowl with blade in position, and pulse 8 times or until coarsely chopped. Carefully remove blade. Scoop the strawberries into a colander; measure 1¼ cups, reserve and set the remaining strawberries aside.

3 Place oil, milk, sour cream, sugar, flour, baking powder, salt, vanilla and egg into the 40-oz. bowl with blade in position, and process for 10 seconds. Remove lid and carefully scrape down the sides of the bowl with a thin rubber spatula. Replace lid and process for 5 to 8 seconds or until well mixed. Carefully remove blade. Add the measured strawberries and fold them in with a spatula until well mixed. Pour the mixture into the prepared muffin pan, filling about ¾ full.

4 Bake for 30 to 40 minutes or until a wooden pick inserted in the center comes out clean. Cool completely before serving.

5 Serve with the extra chopped strawberries on the side.

TIP...

Substitute chopped raspberries for the same amount of chopped strawberries, or use 1½ cups of fresh blueberries but do not chop them.

A word from Bob...

Always check your baked goods about 10 minutes before the recipe says they will be done. Then you will see if your oven bakes a little faster or not.

Cranberry Lemon Scones

Prep: 20 min. **Cook:** 16 min. **Serves:** 8
40-oz. bowl with blade attachment

Instead of being dry and heavy like many in the market, these scones are light and moist even four days later.—Bob

Shopping List

1¾ cups all-purpose flour

⅛ teaspoon salt

¼ cup sugar

1 tablespoon plus 1½ teaspoons baking powder

Zest of 1 lemon

½ stick cold butter, cut into ½-inch cubes

½ cup milk

2 tablespoons heavy whipping cream

½ cup dried cranberries

1 Preheat the oven to 375°.

2 Place flour, salt, sugar, baking powder and lemon zest into the Ninja 40-oz. bowl with blade in position, and pulse 4 times. Remove lid and add the butter. Replace lid and pulse until mixture is coarse and crumbly. Pour the milk and heavy cream through the pour spout, and pulse 10 to 12 times, or until mixture is just combined (do not overmix). Carefully remove blade.

3 Scoop batter onto a lightly floured surface and sprinkle with cranberries. Knead 10 times. Form the dough into a 1-inch thick circle. Cut crosswise to make 8 triangles. Place scones, 1½ inches apart, on a baking sheet lined with aluminum foil.

4 Bake for 16 to 18 minutes or until light golden brown.

TIP...
Switch any other dried fruit for the cranberries in the same amount and of the same size. Store scones in an airtight container for up to 4 days.

CRANBERRY LEMON SCONES

Anytime Crêpes

Prep: 8 min. **Chill:** 20 min. **Cook:** 15 min.
Serves: 10 **40-oz. bowl with blade attachment**

This French delicacy can be used for sweet or savory dishes. For breakfast sprinkle with powdered sugar and lemon juice, and serve with fresh fruit.—Bob

Shopping List

1 cup whole milk

1 cup all-purpose flour

1 teaspoon sugar

¼ teaspoon salt

3 eggs

2 tablespoons unsalted butter, melted

1 Place milk, flour, sugar, salt, eggs and butter into the Ninja 40-oz. bowl with blade in position, and pulse 12 to 15 times or until well mixed. Carefully remove blade. Refrigerate the mixture for 20 minutes.

2 Spray a 10-inch skillet or a crêpe pan with cooking spray. Heat the pan over medium heat. Scoop ¼ cup of crêpe mixture into the hot pan, tilting the pan with a circular motion so that the batter coats the bottom surface evenly.

3 Cook over medium heat for about 1 minute, until the bottom is light brown. Loosen with a spatula, turn and cook the other side. Serve immediately.

TIP...

The batter will keep for up to 48 hours in the refrigerator. For a savory twist add 2 tablespoons chopped fresh herb to the batter.

Almond Waffle

Prep: 10 min. **Cook:** 12 min. **Serves:** 4
40-oz. bowl with blade attachment

These light and fluffy waffles are my family's favorites, especially for Mother's Day brunch. They go well with all the assorted toppings each family member prefers on their waffle.—Andrea

Shopping List

1 cup whole milk

¼ cup unsalted butter, melted

1½ cups all-purpose flour

1¼ teaspoons baking powder

½ teaspoon salt

2 eggs

¾ teaspoon almond extract

1 Place milk, butter, flour, baking powder, salt, eggs and almond extract into the Ninja 40-oz. bowl with blade in position, and pulse 4 times, then process until well mixed. Carefully remove blade.

2 To make the waffles, follow the instructions from your waffle maker.

TIP...

For a little extra texture and flavor fold a ½ cup of toasted sliced almonds into the batter before cooking. If you don't like almond extract, you can substitute another favorite extract.

Dutch Baby Pancake

Prep: 10 min. **Cook:** 20 min. **Serves:** 2
40-oz. bowl with blade attachment

A simple sweet oven-baked pancake inspired by a German apple pancake, thought to originate in the early 1900's in Seattle, Washington. Here's my version.—Andrea

Shopping List

2 large eggs

½ cup whole milk

½ cup bread flour

½ teaspoon vanilla extract

¼ teaspoon ground cinnamon

1½ teaspoons sugar

1 tablespoon butter

1 Place the eggs, milk, flour, vanilla, cinnamon and sugar into the Ninja 40-oz. bowl with blade in position, and pulse 12 to 15 times or until well mixed. Carefully remove blade.

2 Preheat the oven to 425°.

3 Place a 10-inch cast-iron skillet into the oven for 10 minutes or until hot.

4 Remove skillet. Add the butter and stir to melt. Pour in the batter. Place in the oven on the middle rack.

5 Bake for 20 to 22 minutes or until the edges are golden brown and puffy.

TIP...

Do not open the oven while baking. Also, this can be served with the Apple Compote (page 159) or simply topped with confectioners' sugar and lemon.

Healthy Grains Pancake

Prep: 12 min. **Cook:** 10 min. **Serves:** 5
40-oz. bowl with blade attachment

My passion for pancakes drove me to come up with a healthier version full of fiber and healthy fats.—Stephen

Shopping List

1 cup low-fat milk

1 tablespoon plus 1 teaspoon vegetable oil

½ cup all-purpose flour

½ cup whole-wheat flour

½ cup old-fashioned oats

¼ cup loosely packed light brown sugar

½ teaspoon salt

2 teaspoons baking powder

⅓ cup toasted pecans

2 eggs

1 Place milk, oil, flours, oats, brown sugar, salt, baking powder, pecans and eggs into the Ninja 40-oz. bowl with blade in position, and process until well mixed. Carefully remove blade.

2 Preheat an 8-inch skillet over medium heat. Lightly spray with cooking spray.

3 Pour 1¾ ounces of batter into the skillet. Turn over when bubbles form on top. Cook until second side is light golden brown. Repeat for remaining pancakes.

TIP...

Substitute your favorite toasted nuts for the pecans if you prefer.

South American Corn Pancakes

Prep: 14 min. **Cook:** 12 min. **Serves:** 8
40-oz. bowl with blade attachment

I remember these in Venezuela and how different they were from pancakes in the United States. They are served filled, and are never topped with syrup!—Andrea

Shopping List

1 cup all-purpose flour

1 cup cornmeal

1 tablespoon sugar

¼ teaspoon salt

¼ teaspoon baking powder

2 eggs

1 (16-ounce) can creamed corn

¾ cup milk

1 tablespoon vegetable oil

¾ cup frozen corn kernels, thawed

1 Place the flour, cornmeal, sugar, salt, baking powder, eggs, creamed corn, milk and oil into the Ninja 40-oz. bowl with blade in position, and process for 20 seconds or until well mixed. Carefully remove blade. Fold in the corn kernels.

2 Preheat your favorite pancake pan. Spray the pan with cooking spray.

3 Place 2 tablespoons of corn mixture in the hot pan to make pancakes. Cook until lightly browned on both sides.

TIP...

Layer a pancake with mozzarella cheese then another pancake. Top with your favorite jam, butter or even better, shredded pork.

My "Go-To" Cornbread

Prep: 14 min. **Cook:** 35 min.
Cool: 15 min. **Serves:** 8
40-oz. bowl with blade attachment

My ideal breakfast is eggs, bacon and a piece of fresh cornbread. I also like it on its own, fresh out of the oven with butter, or with chili or as a topping on your favorite casserole.—Bob

Shopping List

1 cup buttermilk

⅓ cup vegetable or olive oil

½ cup sugar

1 teaspoon salt

1 cup yellow cornmeal

1 cup all-purpose flour

1 teaspoon baking soda

1 egg

⅓ cup frozen corn kernels, thawed

1 Preheat oven to 350°.

2 Lightly spray a 9-inch round cake pan with cooking spray.

3 Place buttermilk, oil, sugar, salt, cornmeal, flour, baking soda and egg into the Ninja 40-oz. bowl with blade in position, and process for 15 to 20 seconds or until well mixed. Carefully remove blade. Stir in corn with a spatula until evenly mixed. Pour mixture into prepared pan.

4 Bake for 35 to 40 minutes, or until a wooden pick inserted in the center comes out clean.

5 Cool for 15 minutes before serving.

Baked Apple Pastries

Prep: 45 min. **Chill:** 30 minutes   **Cook:** 40 min. **Cool:** 15 min. **Serves:** 12
40-oz. bowl with slicer attachment

Individual pastry pockets that taste just like heaven, a little sweet, a little tart. I love to eat them for breakfast with a latte.—Stephen

Shopping List

1 Basic Pie Dough recipe (page 107)

9 tablespoons sugar, divided

3 tablespoons all-purpose flour

½ teaspoon ground cinnamon

⅛ teaspoon ground nutmeg

2 tablespoons orange juice

Zest of ½ lemon

2 Granny Smith apples, peeled, cored and cut into quarters

1 Golden Delicious apple. peeled, cored and cut into quarters

⅓ cup heavy cream

TIP...

You can use pears instead of apples. It is better to make the dough the day before you are making the pastries and store it in the refrigerator overnight.

A word from Bob...

If you keep pastry dough in your freezer, you can have these homemade treats even more often.

1 Make the Basic Pie Dough recipe, and wrap into 2 separate discs; refrigerate.

2 Preheat the oven to 375°. Line a baking sheet with aluminum foil. Lightly spray with cooking spray.

3 Place 5 tablespoons sugar, flour, cinnamon and nutmeg in a small bowl.

4 Pour orange juice and lemon zest in a medium bowl.

5 Slice the apples into the Ninja 40-oz. bowl with the slicer attachment in position. Place apples on a cutting board and roughly chop. Add apples to the orange juice and zest. Toss to mix well. Sprinkle flour mixture on apples and toss until well mixed.

6 Roll each pie dough disc, separately, on a heavily floured surface into a 10x15-inch rectangle. Cut each into 6 (5x5-inch) squares. Divide apple filling evenly among the 12 squares, placing the filling in the middle of each square. Brush the edges with a little water and fold each corner onto the center of the square, slightly overlapping them. Place pastries onto prepared pan. Refrigerate for 30 minutes.

7 Remove pastries from the refrigerator, brush with heavy cream and sprinkle with the remaining sugar, about 1 teaspoon per pastry.

8 Bake for 30 to 40 minutes or until golden brown. Cool for 15 minutes before serving.

Breakfast Chorizo Burritos

Prep: 15 min. **Cook:** 6 min. **Serves:** 4
40-oz. bowl with blade attachment

This burrito has a slight twist and extra nutrition with a sweet potato in the filling to get you off to a great start for the day.—Stephen

Shopping List

½ large green bell pepper, cut into chunks

½ medium onion, cut into chunks

3½ ounces smoked chorizo, cut into 1-inch pieces

1 medium cooked sweet potato, peeled and cut into chunks

2 teaspoons oil

4 eggs, beaten

¼ cup salsa

¼ teaspoon salt

⅛ teaspoon ground black pepper

8 (6-inch) flour tortillas, warmed

Salsa

Avocado slices

1 Place bell pepper, onion, chorizo and sweet potato in the Ninja 40-oz. bowl with blade in position, and pulse 5 times or until coarsely chopped. Carefully remove blade.

2 Pour the oil into a skillet and heat. Add chorizo mixture and cook for 3 minutes or until hot. Stir in eggs, salsa, salt and pepper. Cook over medium-high heat about 3 minutes or until eggs are set, stirring frequently.

3 Serve egg mixture with warm tortillas, additional salsa and avocado slices.

Turkey Kielbasa Breakfast Casserole

Prep: 15 min. **Cook:** 40 min. **Serves:** 6
40-oz. bowl with blade attachment

Prepared garlic bread is featured in this breakfast casserole. It is quick to put together for breakfast or brunch.—Bob

Shopping List

1 (10-ounce) loaf frozen garlic bread, baked, cooled, cut into 2-inch pieces

6 ounces turkey kielbasa, cut into 1½-inch pieces

1 medium onion, cut into chunks

4 ounces Cheddar cheese, cut into cubes

6 eggs

2½ cups milk

1 teaspoon each: Italian seasoning and paprika

½ teaspoon salt

¼ teaspoon ground black pepper

1 Preheat oven to 350°. Lightly spray a 13x9-inch glass baking dish.

2 Spread garlic bread pieces into dish.

3 Place kielbasa, onion and cheese in the Ninja 40-oz. bowl with blade in position, and pulse 6 times or until coarsely chopped. Carefully remove blade. Pour mixture over the garlic bread.

4 Place remaining ingredients in the 40-oz. bowl with blade in position, and process for 6 seconds. Pour over kielbasa mixture, and press with fork to cover the bread.

5 Bake uncovered at 350° for 40 to 45 minutes or until lightly browned and set in the center.

Spinach and Ricotta Pockets

Prep: 45 min. **Chill:** 30 min. **Cook:** 30 min. **Cool:** 10 min. **Serves:** 12
40-oz. bowl with blade attachment

Every bakery in my country has these pockets. They are made fresh every morning and eaten for breakfast. We all like to believe they are healthy because they have calcium, protein and vegetables and are light and flaky.—Andrea

Shopping List

1 Basic Pie Dough recipe (page 107)

8 ounces whole milk ricotta

3 egg yolks

4 ounces thawed frozen chopped spinach, well drained

1 teaspoon sugar

1 teaspoon salt

½ teaspoon ground black pepper

8 ounces shredded mozzarella cheese

⅓ cup heavy cream

TIP...

After baked and cooled, wrap the pastries individually in plastic wrap and freeze. Thaw overnight in the refrigerator and bake for 10 to 15 minutes at 250° or until warmed.

A word from Bob...

Add a couple of cooked, chopped slices of bacon or 2 ounces of cooked, chopped ham for a great taste addition.

1 Make the Basic Pie Dough recipe and wrap into 2 separate discs; refrigerate.

2 Preheat oven to 375°. Line a baking sheet with aluminum foil. Lightly spray with cooking spray.

3 To make the filling, place ricotta, egg yolks, drained spinach, sugar, salt and pepper into the Ninja 40-oz. bowl with blade in position, and process until well mixed. Carefully remove blade. Add the mozzarella cheese and mix with a spatula until well mixed.

4 Roll each refrigerated pie dough disc on a heavily floured surface, separately, into a 10x15-inch rectangle. Cut each rectangle into 6 (5x5-inch) squares. Divide the filling evenly among the 12 squares, placing filling in the middle. Brush edges with a little water and fold each corner into the center of the square, lightly overlapping the corners. Place pastries onto prepared pan. Refrigerate for 30 minutes.

5 Remove the pastries from the refrigerator. Brush each pastry with the heavy cream.

6 Bake for 30 to 40 minutes or until golden brown. Cool for 10 minutes before serving.

BREAKFAST & THE BAKERY

Chicken Hash

Prep: 20 min. **Cook:** 20 min. **Serves:** 8
40-oz. bowl with blade attachment

This is my healthy recipe for breakfast hash. It has fewer calories and less fat than the traditional version and no canned products. Make it the day before and store it in the refrigerator.—Bob

Shopping List

¼ red onion

½ red bell pepper

2 cloves garlic, peeled

1 pound red skin potatoes,
     cut in half and cooked

¾ pound raw chicken breast

2 tablespoons extra virgin olive oil

⅔ cup vegetable stock

1 teaspoon dried thyme

1 teaspoon salt

1 teaspoon ground black pepper

2 teaspoons paprika

¼ cup fresh parsley leaves

1 Place the onion, red pepper and garlic into the Ninja 40-oz. bowl with blade in position, and pulse 6 times. Carefully remove blade. Place onion mixture in a small bowl.

2 Place the cooked potatoes into the 40-oz. bowl with blade in position, and pulse 8 times. Carefully remove blade. Place potatoes in another bowl.

3 Place the raw chicken breast in the 40-oz. bowl with blade in position, and pulse 8 to 10 times or until evenly chopped. Carefully remove blade.

4 Pour oil in a large sauté pan and heat over medium high. Add the onion mixture.

5 Cook for 4 minutes, stirring occasionally. Stir in the chicken breast, vegetable stock, thyme, salt and pepper.

6 Cook for 5 minutes. Add the potatoes, paprika and parsley, and continue to cook for 10 minutes, stirring occasionally.

Shortbread Cookies

Prep: 11 min. **Chill:** 1 hour
Cook: 13 min. **Yield:** 2½ dozen
40-oz. bowl with cookie paddle attachment

These light, buttery, melt-in-your-mouth cookies are great as a snack with a cup of coffee. Delicious when frosted.—Bob

Shopping List

2 (4-ounce) sticks unsalted butter, softened

⅔ cup confectioners' sugar

2 teaspoons pure vanilla extract

2 cups all-purpose flour

1. Place butter, sugar, vanilla and flour into the Ninja 40-oz. bowl with the cookie paddle in position, and process for 15 seconds. Remove the lid and carefully scrape down the sides of the bowl with a thin rubber spatula. Replace the lid and process for 8 more seconds. Remove cookie paddle. Scoop dough onto plastic wrap, pressing down to form a disc. Wrap and refrigerate for 1 hour.

2. Preheat the oven to 350°.

3. Roll dough on a heavily floured surface, rotating the dough so it doesn't stick, to ¼-inch thickness. Cut cookies with any medium-size cookie cutters. Place them onto a nonstick cookie sheet. Knead the scraps together and roll to cut more cookies.

4. Bake for 11 to 13 minutes or until light golden brown.

TIP...
If the dough is too soft after gathering the scraps, refrigerate for a few minutes before rolling.

Peanut Butter Cookies

Prep: 12 min. **Cook:** 11 min. **Yield:** 2 dozen
40-oz. bowl with cookie paddle attachment

Any peanut butter fan will find these soft but crumbly, chewy but crispy cookies to be the perfect combination of sweet and salty.—Stephen

Shopping List

1 cup creamy peanut butter

1 (4-ounce) stick unsalted butter, softened

1½ teaspoons pure vanilla extract

¾ cup firmly packed light brown sugar

½ cup white sugar

⅛ teaspoon salt

1 cup all-purpose flour

½ teaspoon baking soda

1 large egg, lightly beaten

1. Preheat the oven to 300°.

2. Place peanut butter, butter, vanilla, sugars, salt, flour, baking soda and egg into the Ninja 40-oz. bowl with the cookie paddle in position, and process for 10 seconds. Remove the lid and carefully scrape down the sides of the bowl with a thin rubber spatula. Replace the lid and process for 5 more seconds. Remove cookie paddle. Scoop cookie dough by tablespoons onto a nonstick cookie sheet about 2 inches apart.

3. Bake for 11 to 13 minutes or until cookies are lightly browned.

TIP...
For some extra peanut flavor, stir in ¾ cup of peanut butter chips to the dough before baking.

White Chocolate Macadamia Cookies

Prep: 8 min. **Cook:** 12 min. **Yield:** 2 dozen
40-oz. bowl with cookie paddle attachment

These cookies are sweet and chewy because of the white chocolate, and salty and crunchy with the macadamia nuts. Both tastes create a perfect balance.—Stephen

Shopping List

6 tablespoons unsalted butter, softened

1½ teaspoons pure vanilla extract

½ cup firmly packed light brown sugar

¼ cup white sugar

⅛ teaspoon salt

1 cup plus 2 tablespoons all-purpose flour

¼ teaspoon baking soda

1 large egg, lightly beaten

½ cup white chocolate chips

¾ cup coarsely chopped macadamia nuts

1 Preheat oven to 325°.

2 Place butter, vanilla, sugars, salt, flour, baking soda and egg into the Ninja 40-oz. bowl with the cookie paddle in position, and process for 15 seconds. Remove lid and carefully scrape down the sides of the bowl with a thin rubber spatula. Add chocolate chips and nuts. Replace the lid and pulse 10 more times. Remove cookie paddle and stir until well mixed.

3 Scoop cookie dough by tablespoons onto a nonstick cookie sheet about 2 inches apart.

4 Bake for 10 to 12 minutes or until light golden brown.

Spice-Me-Up Cookies

Prep: 15 min. **Cook:** 13 min. **Yield:** 2 dozen
40-oz. bowl with cookie paddle attachment

These are the perfect cookies for the holiday season with a cup of hot chocolate for the kids, or a cup of eggnog for the adults.—Bob

Shopping List

1 (4-ounce) stick unsalted butter, softened

¾ cup plus 2 tablespoons sugar, divided

¼ teaspoon salt

1⅓ cups all-purpose flour

1 teaspoon cream of tartar

½ teaspoon baking soda

¼ teaspoon ground nutmeg

1 large egg, lightly beaten

1 teaspoon cinnamon

1 Preheat oven to 350°.

2 Place butter, ¾ cup white sugar, salt, flour, cream of tartar, baking soda, nutmeg and egg into the Ninja 40-oz. bowl with cookie paddle in position, and process for 15 seconds. Remove the lid and carefully scrape down the sides of the bowl with a thin rubber spatula. Replace the lid and pulse 5 times. Remove cookie paddle and stir dough with a spatula until well mixed.

3 Mix cinnamon and remaining 2 table-spoons sugar in a medium bowl.

4 Scoop cookie dough by tablespoons, shape into balls, and toss them in the cinnamon-sugar mixture until fully coated. Place dough balls onto a nonstick cookie sheet about 2 inches apart, and lightly flatten.

5 Bake for 11 to 13 minutes or until light golden brown.

Oatmeal Raisin Cookies

Prep: 11 min. **Cook:** 10 min. **Yield:** 2 dozen
40-oz. bowl with cookie paddle attachment

My nieces love the combination of oats, raisins and cinnamon. They always try to trick me into serving these for breakfast because it tastes just like oatmeal.—Andrea

Shopping List

1 (4-ounce) stick unsalted butter, softened

1 teaspoon pure vanilla extract

⅓ cup firmly packed light brown sugar

¼ cup white sugar

¼ teaspoon salt

¾ cup all-purpose flour

½ teaspoon baking soda

¾ teaspoon ground cinnamon

1½ cups old-fashioned rolled oats

1 large egg, lightly beaten

¾ cup raisins

1 Preheat the oven to 350°.

2 Place butter, vanilla, sugars, salt, flour, baking soda, cinnamon, oats and egg into the Ninja 40-oz. bowl with the cookie paddle in position, and process for 15 seconds. Remove the lid and carefully scrape down the sides of the bowl with a thin rubber spatula. Add the raisins, replace the lid and process for 5 to 10 more seconds. Remove cookie paddle and stir with a spatula until raisins are well mixed.

3 Scoop cookie dough by tablespoons onto a nonstick cookie sheet about 2 inches apart.

4 Bake for 8 to 10 minutes or until light golden brown.

Loaded Chocolate Chunk Cookies

Prep: 9 min. **Cook:** 8 min. **Yield:** 2 dozen
40-oz. bowl with cookie paddle attachment

There is nothing like the memory of a warm chocolate chunk cookie. Soft and gooey on the inside, crispy on the outside.—Stephen

Shopping List

1 (4-ounce) stick unsalted butter, softened

1 teaspoon pure vanilla extract

½ cup firmly packed light brown sugar

¼ cup white sugar

½ teaspoon salt

1½ cups all-purpose flour

½ teaspoon baking soda

1 large egg, lightly beaten

1¼ cups semisweet chocolate chunks

1 Preheat the oven to 350°.

2 Place butter, vanilla, sugars, salt, flour, baking soda and egg into the Ninja 40-oz. bowl with the cookie paddle in position, and process for 15 seconds. Remove the lid and carefully scrape down the sides of the bowl with a thin rubber spatula. Add the chocolate chunks. Replace the lid and pulse 10 times. Remove cookie paddle. Stir with a spatula until the chocolate chunks are well mixed. Scoop cookie dough by tablespoons onto a nonstick cookie sheet about 2 inches apart.

3 Bake for 8 to 10 minutes until light golden brown.

TIP...

If you don't have nonstick cookie sheets, just line regular pans with parchment paper.

Double Chocolate Chip Cookies

Prep: 10 min. **Cook:** 12 min. **Yield:** 2 dozen
40-oz. bowl with cookie paddle attachment

These cookies are softer than a regular cookie and are in the traditional shape of a chocolate chunk cookie. But they taste more like a brownie!—Stephen

Shopping List

1 (4-ounce) stick unsalted butter, softened

1 teaspoon pure vanilla extract

½ cup firmly packed light brown sugar

⅓ cup white sugar

¼ teaspoon salt

1¼ cups all-purpose flour

¼ cup sifted cocoa powder

¼ teaspoon baking soda

2 large eggs, lightly beaten

1¼ cups semisweet chocolate chunks

1 Preheat oven to 325°.

2 Place butter, vanilla, sugars, salt, flour, cocoa, baking soda and eggs into the Ninja 40-oz. bowl with the cookie paddle in position, and process for 15 seconds. Remove the lid and carefully scrape down the sides of the bowl with a thin rubber spatula. Add the chocolate chunks. Replace the lid and pulse 10 times. Remove cookie paddle and stir with a spatula until the chocolate chunks are well mixed. Scoop cookie dough by tablespoons onto a nonstick cookie sheet about 2 inches apart.

3 Bake for 10 to 12 minutes until light golden brown.

TIPS...

For a black and white creation with a little more sweetness, use white chocolate chunks instead of the semisweet.

My Sweet Pastry Dough

Prep: 16 min. **Chill:** 4 hours **Yield:** 1 single 9-inch crust with lattice top
40-oz. bowl with dough blade attachment

This is a pie dough recipe that is impossible to overmix because of the ratio of ingredients. It's tender, sweet and crumbly and can be used with sweet or savory fillings.—Bob

Shopping List

2 cups all-purpose flour

¼ teaspoon salt

½ teaspoon baking powder

⅓ cup sugar

4 tablespoons (2 ounces) cold unsalted butter, cut into ½-inch cubes

5 tablespoons (2 ounces) cold shortening, cut into ½-inch cubes

2 large eggs, lightly beaten

1 Place flour, salt, baking powder and sugar into the Ninja 40-oz. bowl with dough blade in position, and pulse 5 times. Remove the lid. Add the butter and shortening. Replace the lid and pulse 6 times. Remove the lid and dough blade. Add the eggs and stir until just combined and a dough ball forms. Dough will be a little sticky. Scoop out dough onto a lightly floured surface and softly knead, folding dough over itself 6 to 8 times.

2 Dough can be rolled and used right away, or it can formed into a flattened 1-inch thick disc, wrapped with plastic wrap and refrigerated for 4 hours (up to 4 days or until ready to use).

Seasoned Flat Bread

Prep: 8 min. **Rise:** 2 hours **Cook:** 20 min. **Serves:** 4
40-oz. bowl with dough blade attachment

This recipe is a great substitute for regular dinner rolls when having an Italian meal.—Stephen

Shopping List

2 cups unbleached bread flour

1 (¼-ounce) package active dry yeast

1 tablespoon plus 1 teaspoon sugar

1 teaspoon salt

⅔ cup warm water (115° to 120°)

2 tablespoons extra virgin olive oil

1 tablespoon Italian seasoning

⅓ cup grated Parmesan cheese

1 Place flour, yeast, sugar and salt into the Ninja 40-oz. bowl with the dough blade in position, and pulse 5 times. Add the water and olive oil and pulse 10 times. Add the seasoning and cheese and process until it forms a uniform ball (about 50 seconds). Carefully remove dough blade. Place the dough ball In a lightly greased bowl. Cover loosely with plastic wrap and let rise for 2 hours.

2 Preheat the oven to 350°.

3 Lightly spray a 17x11x1-inch baking sheet with cooking spray. Spread dough onto baking sheet.

4 Bake for 20 to 30 minutes or until light golden brown.

TIP...

To make 8 dinner rolls, shape and bake at the same temperature in a baking pan lined with parchment paper for 25 to 35 minutes.

SEASONED FLAT BREAD

BASIC WHITE BREAD DOUGH

Basic White Bread Dough

Prep: 8 min. **Rise:** 2 hours **Cook:** 30 min.
40-oz. bowl with dough blade attachment

This recipe is so versatile you could create a pizza or just serve with your favorite meal.—Stephen

Shopping List

2 cups unbleached bread flour

1 (¼-ounce) package active dry yeast

1 tablespoon plus 1 teaspoon white sugar

1 teaspoon salt

6 ounces warm water (115° to 120°)

2 tablespoons extra virgin olive oil

1 Place flour, yeast, sugar, salt, water and oil into the Ninja 40-oz. bowl with dough blade in position, and pulse 5 times, then process until it forms a uniform ball (about 20 to 25 seconds). Carefully remove dough blade.

2 Place the dough ball In a lightly greased bowl. Cover loosely with plastic wrap and let rise for 2 hours.

3 **For dinner rolls**, preheat oven to 350°.

4 Divide dough into 8 equal-size balls. Place on a baking sheet lined with parchment paper and brush lightly with olive oil.

5 Bake for 25 to 35 minutes.

6 **For pizza**, preheat oven to 400°.

7 Lightly spray a 12-inch pizza pan with cooking spray. Roll or spread dough onto pan. Cover with Pizza Sauce (page 78) and top with your favorite toppings.

8 Bake for 30 to 40 minutes or until lightly browned.

Basic Pie Dough

Prep: 18 min. **Chill:** 4 hours
Yield: 1 double crust or 2 single crusts
40-oz. bowl with dough blade attachment

This "go-to" dough delivers when I want to have a nice, flaky crust for sweet pies or savory pocket pastries.—Andrea

Shopping List

2½ cups all-purpose flour

1¼ teaspoons salt

6 tablespoons (3 ounces) cold unsalted butter, cut into ½-inch cubes

5 tablespoons (5 ounces) cold shortening, cut into ½-inch cubes

½ to ⅔ cup cold water

1 Place flour and salt into the Ninja 40-oz. bowl with dough blade in position, and pulse 5 times. Remove the lid. Add the butter and shortening, and lightly shake the bowl a little to partially coat. Replace the lid and pulse 5 times. Starting with ½ cup water, pour in the water while pulsing 8 to 10 times or until dough pulls together. Add more water as necessary. Do not overmix. Dough will be sticky, crumbly and not fully mixed. Carefully remove dough blade. Scoop out dough on a lightly floured surface and softly knead 3 to 4 times just until mixed. Do not overwork.

2 Divide the dough into 2 equal pieces. Form each piece into a 1-inch flattened disc. Wrap each piece with plastic wrap. Refrigerate 4 hours or overnight.

TIP...

The wrapped discs can be frozen for up to a month. Thaw in the refrigerator for 2 days before using.

Whole-Wheat Pizza Dough

Prep: 8 min. **Rise:** 2 hours **Cook:** 30 min. **Serves:** 8
40-oz. bowl with dough blade attachment

This recipe is a healthier version of regular pizza dough recipes, but with the same flavor and texture.—Bob

Shopping List

1 cup unbleached bread flour

1 cup whole-wheat flour

1 (¼-ounce) package active dry yeast

1 tablespoon plus 1 teaspoon white sugar

1 teaspoon salt

6 ounces warm water (115° to 120°)

2 tablespoons extra virgin olive oil

1 Place flours, yeast, sugar, salt, water and oil into the Ninja 40-oz. bowl with dough blade in position, and pulse 5 times, then process until it forms a uniform ball (about 25 seconds). Carefully remove blade.

2 Place the dough ball in a lightly greased bowl. Cover loosely with plastic wrap and let rise for 2 hours.

3 Preheat the oven to 400°. Lightly spray a 12-inch pizza pan with cooking spray.

4 Roll or spread the dough onto the pan. Cover with Pizza Sauce (page 78) and top with your favorite ingredients.

5 Bake for 30 to 40 minutes or until light golden brown and dough is cooked.

TIP...

If you like really thin pizza dough this recipe can make 2 (10-inch) pizzas.

Old-Fashioned Biscuits

Prep: 9 min. **Cook:** 15 min. **Yield:** 9
40-oz. bowl with blade attachment

*For breakfast with eggs and bacon, for lunch or for dinner with gravy
and fried chicken, I can never get enough of these biscuits.—Bob*

Shopping List

2 cups all-purpose flour

1 tablespoon baking powder

¾ teaspoon salt

2 teaspoons sugar

⅓ cup cold butter-flavored shortening, cut into ½-inch cubes

¾ cup whole milk

¼ cup heavy whipping cream

1 Preheat the oven to 425°.

2 Place flour, baking powder, salt and sugar into the Ninja 40-oz. bowl with
blade in position, and pulse 3 times. Add cold shortening and pulse 7 times
or until mixture resembles coarse crumbs. Pour in milk and cream and pulse
9 times. Do not overmix. Dough will be sticky. Carefully remove blade.

3 Scoop the dough onto a lightly floured surface. Knead the dough 10 times
until well mixed. Flatten the dough to a ¾-inch thickness. Cut circles using
a 2-inch round cutter. Press scraps together and keep cutting until all the
dough is used. Place biscuits in a baking sheet lined with foil.

4 Bake for 15 minutes.

TIP...
*Brush the biscuits
with melted butter as
soon as they come out
of the oven for a little
extra butter flavor.*

SHRIMP AND WHITE BEAN SOUP   P 112

Soups & Sides

The warming aroma of home-made soup in the winter is very special indeed. Savor the taste of Loaded Cauliflower Soup (page 116), which captures the trend towards mashed cauliflower instead of mashed potatoes—your family will hardly know the difference.

Side dishes are no longer an afterthought with these quick-to-put-together recipes. Enjoy the excellent combo of parsnips and carrots in Parsnip Carrot Purée (page 128) or the classic southern favorite Corn Pudding (page 128).

Included in this chapter...

SOUPS & SIDES

A word from Bob...

It has never been easier to "round out" your menu by adding a great-tasting soup or side dish and encouraging your family to enjoy more vegetables.

111

Shrimp and White Bean Soup

Prep: 20 min. **Cook:** 30 min. **Serves:** 5
40-oz. bowl with blade attachment

Years ago as a restaurant chef, I created dinner appetizers with beans and shrimp. I blended these together and created a soup inspired by my past.—Andrea

Shopping List

½ medium yellow onion

1 carrot, peeled

1 stalk celery

1 tablespoon extra virgin olive oil

1 (28-ounce) can diced tomatoes, undrained

2 (15-ounce) cans cannellini beans, drained and rinsed

3 cloves garlic, peeled

1 teaspoon Italian seasoning

½ teaspoon crushed red pepper

2 cups chicken broth

½ teaspoon salt

½ teaspoon ground black pepper

8 ounces cooked baby shrimp

1 Place the onion, carrot and celery into the Ninja 40-oz. bowl with blade in position, and pulse 8 times. Carefully remove blade.

2 Place the oil and vegetable mixture in a 5-quart saucepan.

3 Cook over medium heat 5 minutes, or until the vegetables are softened, stirring occasionally.

4 Stir in the tomatoes, beans, garlic, Italian seasoning, red pepper, broth, salt and pepper.

5 Cook over medium heat 20 minutes, or until heated through, stirring occasionally.

6 Remove half of the soup and pour into the 40-oz. bowl with blade in position, and process for 15 seconds. Carefully remove blade. Return the mixture back to the saucepan and add the shrimp.

7 Cook over medium heat an additional 4 minutes, or until shrimp are heated, stirring occasionally.

SOUPS
& SIDES

Chicken Corn Tortilla Soup

Prep: 20 min. **Cook:** 35 min. **Serves:** 5
40-oz bowl with blade attachment

Classic tortilla soup you'll find in Mexico combines fresh corn, roasted tomatoes, homemade chicken broth, seasonings and crispy tortillas. It is very rich and vibrant with lasting aromas. This recipe is simpler yet stays true to the Mexican cuisine.—Andrea

Shopping List

½ medium yellow onion

1 clove garlic, peeled

1 stalk celery

1 tablespoon vegetable oil

1 (14-ounce) can whole peeled tomatoes, drained

1½ pounds boneless skinless chicken thighs, cut into small pieces

1½ cups frozen corn kernels

2½ cups chicken stock

5 ounces enchilada sauce

1 (10-ounce) can diced tomatoes with green chiles

1 teaspoon light chili powder

½ teaspoon cumin

½ teaspoon salt

½ teaspoon ground black pepper

½ cup crushed corn tortilla chips

5 teaspoons chopped fresh cilantro

1 Place the onion, garlic and celery into the Ninja 40-oz. bowl with blade in position, and process for 15 seconds. Carefully remove blade.

2 Heat the oil in a large saucepan over medium-high heat. Stir in the onion mixture.

3 Cook for 4 minutes, stirring occasionally.

4 Place the peeled tomatoes in the 40-oz. bowl with blade in position, and process for 10 seconds. Carefully remove blade.

5 Add the tomatoes, chicken thighs, corn, chicken stock, enchilada sauce, tomatoes with chiles, chili powder, cumin, salt and pepper to the saucepan.

6 Cook over medium heat 30 minutes, stirring occasionally.

7 Divide the soup among 5 soup bowls and top with the tortilla chips and cilantro.

TIP...
Top this soup with slices of avocado and freshly squeezed lime juice for a daring new taste.

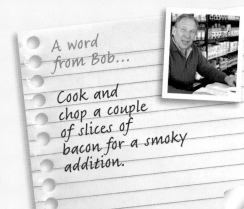

A word from Bob...

Cook and chop a couple of slices of bacon for a smoky addition.

Beer Cheese Soup

Prep: 18 min. **Cook:** 30 min. **Serves:** 4
40-oz. bowl with blade attachment

Beer and cheese remind me of an afternoon watching football with friends and of fishing trips to the lake house. Since I always have these two ingredients on hand, when I want to remember those cold afternoons with my friends, I whip up this soup and it takes me back.—Stephen

Shopping List

1 stalk celery

½ medium yellow onion, peeled

1 carrot, peeled

1 clove garlic, peeled

3 tablespoons unsalted butter

3 tablespoons all-purpose flour

1 cup chicken stock

1 (12-ounce) bottle lager beer

2 dashes hot pepper sauce

1 tablespoon Worcestershire sauce

5 ounces smoked beef sausage

½ cup whole milk

4 ounces Pepper Jack cheese

TIP...

Serve the soup in four scooped-out individual sourdough round bread loaves, which have been warmed in a 350° oven for 6 minutes. Pour the soup in the bread bowl, and serve with the scooped-out bread for dipping.

1 Place the celery, onion, carrot and garlic into the Ninja 40-oz. bowl with blade in position, and pulse 12 times. Carefully remove blade.

2 Place the butter and celery mixture into a large saucepan.

3 Cook 5 minutes over medium heat, or until vegetables are cooked. Stir in the flour.

4 Cook 3 minutes, or until the flour is lightly browned, stirring occasionally.

5 Stir in the chicken stock, beer, hot sauce and Worcestershire sauce.

6 Cook 15 minutes, or until thickened and hot, stirring occasionally.

7 Place the sausage into the 40-oz. bowl with blade in position, and pulse 10 times. Carefully remove blade.

8 Stir the milk, cheese and sausage into the stock mixture.

9 Cook 5 minutes or until heated through, stirring occasionally.

Broccoli Cheese Soup

Prep: 20 min. **Cook:** 25 min. **Serves:** 5
40-oz. bowl with blade attachment

Broccoli cheese soup is found on many soup and sandwich chain restaurant menus. Whether it's cold outside or you're feeling under the weather, this perfect comfort food is so rich and creamy that it will warm you from head to toe.—Bob

Shopping List

3 tablespoons unsalted butter

½ medium yellow onion, cut into 1-inch pieces

1 head broccoli, cut into florets

3 tablespoons all-purpose flour

2 cups vegetable stock

½ teaspoon salt

½ teaspoon ground black pepper

½ teaspoon garlic powder

¼ cup sour cream

8 ounces shredded Cheddar cheese

TIP...

For a great casserole, mix this soup with 1 pound cooked elbow macaroni, sprinkle with more cheese and bake at 350° for about 18 minutes.

1 Place the butter and onion in a medium saucepan over medium-high heat. Cook 3 minutes or until the onion is tender, stirring occasionally.

2 Stir in the broccoli and cook 2 minutes. Stir in the flour.

3 Cook 2 minutes or until the flour is starting to lightly brown, stirring occasionally.

4 Stir in the vegetable stock, salt, pepper and garlic powder. Bring the mixture to a boil then reduce to a simmer.

5 Cook 10 minutes or until mixture is heated through, stirring occasionally.

6 Stir in the sour cream and cook for 1 minute over low heat.

7 Remove the pan from the heat and let stand 5 minutes.

8 Carefully pour the hot soup into the Ninja 40-oz. bowl with blade in position, and process for 15 seconds. Carefully remove blade.

9 Return the soup to the saucepan. Stir in the cheese and heat 3 minutes, or until the cheese is melted, stirring constantly.

Loaded Cauliflower Soup

Prep: 25 min. **Cook:** 25 min. **Serves:** 5

40-oz. bowl with blade attachment

Cauliflower mashed potatoes are today's trend. It all started by trying to reduce the amount of carbohydrates in the traditional mashed potato side dish. Why not take the same idea and create a low carb soup by using cauliflower?—Bob

Shopping List

1 tablespoon vegetable oil

2 cloves garlic, peeled

¼ medium yellow onion, cut into 1-inch pieces

1 stalk celery, cut into 1-inch pieces

1 head cooked cauliflower, cut into 1-inch pieces

2 cups vegetable stock

6 slices cooked bacon, cut into 1-inch pieces

½ teaspoon salt

½ teaspoon ground black pepper

¼ cup sour cream

½ cup chopped green onions

¾ cup shredded Cheddar cheese

1 Heat the oil in a medium saucepan. Add the garlic, onion, celery and cauliflower.

2 Cook over medium-high heat 5 minutes.

3 Add the stock, bacon, salt and pepper and bring the mixture to a boil. Reduce to a simmer and cook 15 minutes, stirring occasionally.

4 Remove the saucepan from the stove and let stand 5 minutes.

5 Carefully pour the hot soup into the Ninja 40-oz. bowl with blade in position, and process for 15 seconds. Carefully remove blade.

6 Return the soup to the saucepan. Stir in the sour cream.

7 Heat 3 minutes over low heat, stirring occasionally.

8 Divide the soup among 5 soup bowls and top with green onions and cheese.

TIP...

Save a few calories by using nonfat sour cream, low-fat shredded Cheddar cheese and turkey bacon.

Sweet Potato Soup

Prep: 20 min. **Cook:** 45 min. **Serves:** 5
40-oz. bowl with blade attachment

One of my favorite root vegetables is a sweet potato, and the best part is that they are a good source of vitamin A, C and B6. What makes this soup special is that it gets sweetened with maple syrup and has a hint of ginger to give it a kick.—Bob

Shopping List

1 tablespoon vegetable oil

½ medium yellow onion, sliced

1 pound and 6 ounces sweet potatoes, peeled and cut into 1-inch pieces

3 cups chicken stock

2 tablespoons maple syrup

½ teaspoon salt

¼ teaspoon ground ginger

⅛ teaspoon cayenne pepper

½ cup heavy cream

2½ teaspoons chopped fresh chives for garnish

TIP...

For a bolder flavored soup, add ½ teaspoon curry powder, or garnish with crumbled goat cheese and diced apples.

1 Place the oil and onion in a 5-quart saucepan.

2 Cook over medium heat 5 minutes, or until the onion is softened, stirring occasionally.

3 Add the potatoes, stock, maple syrup, salt, ginger and pepper.

4 Cook over medium heat 35 minutes or until the sweet potatoes are tender, stirring occasionally.

5 Stir in the heavy cream and continue to cook for 4 minutes, stirring occasionally.

6 Remove from the heat and let stand 5 minutes.

7 Carefully pour the hot potato soup into the Ninja 40-oz. bowl with blade in position, and process for 15 to 20 seconds. Carefully remove blade.

8 Divide the soup among 5 soup bowls and top each with ½ teaspoon fresh chives.

CHILLED MELON SOUP

Chilled Melon Soup

Prep: 18 min. **Serves:** 5
40-oz. bowl with blade attachment

This chilled soup is light, refreshing, full of flavor, and a healthy way to start a meal on a hot summer day. The best part is you can make it a day in advance and keep it refrigerated until served.—Stephen

Shopping List

½ cantaloupe, cut into 1-inch pieces

1 jalapeño, seeded

1 tablespoon freshly squeezed lime juice

1 tablespoon honey

1 cucumber, seeded

¼ teaspoon ground ginger

1¾ cups apple juice

½ cup low-fat Greek yogurt

½ teaspoon salt

1 Place cantaloupe, jalapeño, lime juice, honey, cucumber, ginger, apple juice, yogurt and salt into the Ninja 40-oz. bowl with blade in position.

2 Process for 30 seconds until smooth. Carefully remove blade.

TIP...
Substitute honeydew or watermelon for a pleasing change of taste in place of the cantaloupe.

Carrot Ginger Soup

Prep: 8 min. **Cook:** 18 min. **Serves:** 3
40-oz. bowl with blade attachment

This simple-to-make soup takes little time to prepare and is really healthy . . . packed with vitamin A and beta carotene. The ginger gives it a little Asian twist.—Andrea

Shopping List

1 cup peeled, cooked carrot slices, cooled

2 small cloves garlic, peeled

¼ medium yellow onion, peeled

2 teaspoons grated fresh ginger

½ teaspoon salt

¼ teaspoon black pepper

1⅓ cups chicken broth

Nonfat Greek yogurt

Thinly sliced green onions

1 Place carrots, garlic, onion, ginger, salt, pepper, and chicken broth in the Ninja 40-oz. bowl with blade in position, and process until smooth. Carefully remove blade.

2 Pour soup into a medium saucepan and bring to a boil. Stir occasionally.

3 To serve, garnish with yogurt and green onions.

TIP...
This soup is also very good served cold. To enhance the sweetness of the garlic and onion, sauté them in a little butter.

Potato Leek Soup

Prep: 20 min. **Cook:** 45 min. **Serves:** 4
40-oz. bowl with blade attachment

Potato and leek is a classic French combination. I like mine topped with a little dollop of nonfat Greek yogurt and fresh chopped chives.—Bob

Shopping List

4 tablespoons unsalted butter

6½ ounces leeks, white and light green parts only, cut lengthwise, washed and coarsely chopped

2 cloves garlic, peeled and chopped

1¼ cups water

1 pound potatoes, peeled and cut into 1-inch pieces

3 cups low-sodium chicken broth

½ teaspoon salt

¾ teaspoon ground black pepper

½ cup heavy whipping cream

1 Place the butter into a 5-quart saucepan. Add leeks and garlic.

2 Cook over low heat 8 to 10 minutes without browning, stirring often. Add water.

3 Cook 15 minutes over low heat until heated through, stirring occasionally. Raise the heat to medium. Stir in potatoes, broth, salt and pepper.

4 Cook 20 minutes or until vegetables are tender.

5 Turn off heat and let the mixture stand 5 minutes.

6 Carefully pour the hot leek mixture into the Ninja 40-oz. bowl with blade in position, and process until smooth. Carefully remove blade.

Ham & Cabbage Soup

Prep: 20 min. **Cook:** 40 min. **Serves:** 4
40-oz. bowl with blade attachment

We spent many holidays at my aunt's house when I was growing up. She was good at using leftovers, like ham.—Andrea

Shopping List

½ medium onion

1 carrot, peeled

¼ head green cabbage

1 ham steak (8 ounces), cut into 9 pieces

1 tablespoon vegetable oil

3 cups chicken stock

½ teaspoon garlic powder

2 teaspoons horseradish

¾ teaspoon salt

¾ teaspoon ground black pepper

¼ teaspoon dry mustard

¼ teaspoon dried thyme

½ cup fresh parsley leaves

1 Place the onion, carrot, cabbage and ham into the Ninja 40-oz. bowl with blade in position (in 3 separate batches), and pulse 10 times. Carefully remove blade.

2 Place the oil and cabbage mixture into a large saucepan.

3 Cook 5 minutes over medium heat, stirring occasionally.

4 Stir in the stock, garlic powder, horseradish, salt, pepper, mustard, thyme, and parsley.

5 Cook 35 minutes over medium-low heat or until heated through and the vegetables are tender, stirring occasionally.

SOUPS
& SIDES

Pizza Soup

Prep: 15 min. **Cook:** 25 min. **Serves:** 5
40-oz. bowl with blade attachment

I like everything pizza. Here is a chunky, hearty soup with a perfect consistency.—Andrea

Shopping List

1 tablespoon vegetable oil

¼ medium yellow onion, sliced

½ medium green bell pepper, chopped

3 cloves garlic, peeled

1 (28-ounce) can diced tomatoes, undrained

4 ounces pepperoni

1½ cups chicken stock

1 tablespoon Italian seasoning

½ teaspoon salt

½ teaspoon ground black pepper

½ cup shredded mozzarella cheese

1 Place the oil, onion, green pepper and garlic in a 5-quart saucepan.

2 Cook over medium heat 5 minutes, or until vegetables soften, stirring occasionally.

3 Stir in tomatoes, pepperoni, stock, seasoning, salt and pepper.

4 Cook over medium heat 20 minutes, or until heated through and vegetables are tender, stirring occasionally.

5 Remove the saucepan from the heat and let stand 10 minutes.

6 Carefully pour hot pepperoni mixture into the Ninja 40-oz. bowl with blade in position, and process for 30 seconds. Carefully remove blade.

7 Top soup with the cheese.

Au Gratin Potatoes

Prep: 15 min. **Cook:** 65 min. **Serves:** 9
40-oz. bowl with slicer attachment

Thinly sliced potatoes layered with cream and covered in cheese is my perfect definition of a side dish. I often make these potatoes with a steak topped with Steak Sauce (page 77) and a green salad with the Italian Vinaigrette (page 64).—Bob

Shopping List

2 pounds medium baking potatoes, washed, but not peeled

¾ teaspoon each: salt and black pepper

1 teaspoon dried thyme

1 cup heavy cream

¾ cup half-and-half

2 tablespoons butter, melted

½ cup shredded Swiss cheese

1 Preheat oven to 350°. Cut the potatoes in half. Slice the potatoes in the Ninja 40-oz. bowl with the slicer attachment in position. Place the potatoes in a medium bowl and toss with the salt, pepper and thyme.

2 Add all the potatoes to an 8x8-inch baking dish. Place cream, half-and-half, and butter in a bowl and mix well. Pour cream mixture over potatoes. Sprinkle evenly with the cheese. Cover the baking pan with parchment paper then aluminum foil.

3 Bake at 350° for 1 hour or until potatoes are tender.

4 Remove the foil and parchment. Broil at 500° for 5 minutes to create a golden brown crust.

AU GRATIN POTATOES

SOUPS
& SIDES

TIP...
You can substitute any cheese for the Swiss cheese.

Broccoli Patties

Prep: 15 min. **Cook:** 40 min. **Chill:** 20 min. **Serves:** 5
40-oz. bowl with blade attachment

While traveling through South America, I discovered different vegetable tortitas, and to my surprise, all the kids loved them. I created my own recipe for my own children to love eating their vegetables!—Andrea

Shopping List

2 medium heads broccoli, cut into florets

½ white onion, peeled

3 cloves garlic, peeled

3 tablespoons unsalted butter

3 tablespoons all-purpose flour

½ teaspoon salt

½ teaspoon ground black pepper

⅛ teaspoon ground nutmeg

6 ounces shredded Swiss cheese

1 cup bread crumbs for coating

¼ cup vegetable oil for frying

1 Bring 3½ quarts of water to a boil in a large pot. Add the broccoli.

2 Cook over medium-high heat 5 to 8 minutes, or until broccoli is tender but still crisp. Do not overcook. Drain completely.

3 Place broccoli florets, in 2 batches, into the Ninja 40-oz. bowl with blade in position, and pulse 6 to 8 times or until broccoli is evenly chopped. Carefully remove blade. Remove broccoli and set aside.

4 Place onion and garlic in the 40-oz. bowl with blade in position, and pulse 5 to 10 times or until finely chopped. Carefully remove blade.

5 Place butter, onion and garlic in the large pot.

6 Cook over medium-low heat 6 minutes or until onions are translucent. Stir in flour, salt, pepper and nutmeg.

7 Cook over medium-low heat 4 minutes, or until flour starts to lightly brown, stirring constantly.

8 Stir in broccoli until fully combined. Remove pot from the heat. Stir in cheese until cheese is melted and well blended. Pour mixture into a bowl, cover and refrigerate 20 minutes.

9 Scoop the broccoli mixture to form 10 balls. Flatten to create patties, and coat with bread crumbs.

10 Pour oil into a 12-inch skillet. Cook 4 patties in the skillet at a time.

11 Cook over medium heat 3 to 4 minutes on each side until golden brown. Repeat with remaining patties. Serve hot.

TIP...
Try substituting your favorite cheese for the Swiss, or cauliflower for the broccoli.

SOUPS & SIDES

Spanish Frittata

Prep: 18 min. **Cook:** 35 min. **Serves:** 6
40-oz. bowl with slicer attachment, blade attachment

This recipe is a much easier version of the original Tortilla Española—a long and complicated process of cooking potatoes in olive oil until tender but not browned, draining, then mixing with eggs, pouring into a skillet and finishing on a stove top, flipping it halfway through.—Andrea

Shopping List

1½ pounds white potatoes, peeled and cut in half lengthwise

1 medium yellow onion, peeled, cut in half

¾ teaspoon salt

½ teaspoon ground black pepper

¼ cup olive oil

8 large eggs

1 Preheat the oven to 425°. Line a jellyroll pan with aluminum foil, and lightly coat foil with cooking spray.

2 With the slicer attachment in position, separately slice potatoes and onion, and place in a large bowl. Add salt, pepper and olive oil, and toss until evenly coated.

3 Place potato mixture onto prepared pan and spread evenly.

4 Bake at 425° for 12 to 14 minutes or until potatoes are almost tender.

5 Pour eggs into the Ninja 40-oz. bowl with blade in position, and process for 15 to 20 seconds. Carefully remove blade.

6 Remove potato mixture from the oven. Reduce oven temperature to 350°.

7 Spray a 10-inch skillet with cooking spray. Place potato mixture into skillet and distribute evenly. Pour eggs slowly into skillet, covering potatoes and onions.

8 Bake at 350° for 20 to 25 minutes or until eggs are set and potatoes are tender.

9 Cool 5 minutes and invert onto a serving plate.

TIP...

Traditionally made a day ahead and eaten cold, this frittata is also great hot from the oven.

SWEET POTATO CASSEROLE

Sweet Potato Casserole

Prep: 16 min. **Cook:** 1 hour 15 min. **Serves:** 12
40-oz. bowl with slicer attachment and blade attachment

Are you tired of eating the same old sweet potato casserole with toasted marshmallows on top? Try the same ingredients presented differently with a more creative topping.—Stephen

Shopping List

2 pounds sweet potatoes, peeled

6 large eggs

16 ounces heavy cream

1 teaspoon salt

1 teaspoon ground black pepper

½ teaspoon vanilla extract

1 cup pecans

¾ cup light brown sugar

½ cup all-purpose flour

½ teaspoon ground cinnamon

½ cup butter, melted

TIP...

To spice it up, use pumpkin pie spice or apple pie spice in place of the cinnamon.

1 Preheat the oven to 350°.

2 Cut the sweet potatoes in half. With the slicer attachment in position, slice the potatoes.

3 Place the eggs, cream, salt, pepper and vanilla in the Ninja 40-oz. bowl with blade in position, and pulse 10 seconds. Carefully remove blade.

4 Place the potatoes in a greased 8 x 11½-inch baking pan. Pour the egg mixture over the potatoes.

5 Bake uncovered at 350° for 1 hour.

6 Place pecans, brown sugar, flour, and cinnamon in the 40-oz. bowl with blade in position, and pulse 5 times. Add the butter and pulse 5 additional times. Carefully remove blade.

7 Remove the baking dish from the oven and crumble the pecan mixture evenly over the top.

8 Bake at 350° for an additional 15 minutes.

Parsnip Carrot Purée

Prep: 18 min. **Cook:** 30 min. **Serves:** 4
40-oz. bowl with blade attachment

Related to the carrot, the parsnip is paler in color and offers a sweeter taste and fragrance. This root vegetable is much higher in vitamins and minerals than its relative.—Bob

Shopping List

10 ounces parsnips, peeled, cut into 2-inch pieces

2 medium carrots (about 5 ounces), peeled, cut into 2-inch pieces

1 cup half-and-half

¾ cup water

3 tablespoons butter

½ teaspoon salt

½ teaspoon ground black pepper

⅛ teaspoon ground coriander

1 Place the peeled parsnips and carrots in a medium saucepan. Stir in the half-and-half, water, butter, salt, pepper and coriander. Bring to a boil, then reduce to a simmer, and continue to cook until the carrots are soft. Strain the parsnips and carrots, reserving the liquid.

2 Place the parsnips and carrots into the Ninja 40-oz. bowl with blade in position. Pour in ¾ cup of the reserved liquid, and process for 20 seconds or until creamy. Carefully remove blade.

TIP...
For a special occasion, add 1 tablespoon truffle oil during the processing.

Corn Pudding

Prep: 10 min. **Cook:** 45 min. **Serves:** 9
40-oz. bowl with blade attachment

This corn pudding recipe is classic Southern cooking, simple and delicious. It is slightly sweet, but overall savory. Serve it with baked ham, ribs or turkey.—Bob

Shopping List

3 cups frozen corn, thawed, divided

3 tablespoons butter

3 tablespoons sugar

2 tablespoons all-purpose flour

½ cup heavy cream

4 large eggs

1 teaspoon baking powder

½ teaspoon salt

½ teaspoon ground black pepper

1 Preheat oven to 350°.

2 Place 2 cups of corn, butter, sugar, flour, cream, eggs, baking powder, salt and pepper into the Ninja 40-oz. bowl with blade in position, and process for 25 seconds. Carefully remove blade.

3 Stir in the remaining 1 cup corn until well mixed. Spread the corn mixture into an 8x8-inch baking dish.

4 Bake at 350° for 45 minutes or until the mixture is set.

TIP...
To make a sweeter version, mix 1 tablespoon melted butter, 1 teaspoon sugar and ¼ teaspoon ground cinnamon to sprinkle on top after baking.

CORN PUDDING

Vegetable Ratatouille

Prep: 20 min. **Cook:** 1 hour 10 min. **Serves:** 12
40-oz. bowl with slicer attachment

A traditional French vegetable side dish often surrounded by much debate about how to make it! Ultimately this dish is popular with dieters since it is low in fat and calories and high in nutrients.—Bob

Shopping List

1 eggplant (about 10 ounces)

12 yellow squash

2 medium red bell peppers (about 8 ounces)

½ yellow onion, peeled

12 zucchini

1 (28-ounce) can diced tomatoes, divided

1 tablespoon dried basil

1 teaspoon dried thyme

1 teaspoon salt

1 teaspoon ground black pepper

1 teaspoon sugar

¼ cup cold water

4 tablespoons tomato paste

2 cloves garlic, peeled

1   Preheat oven to 350°. With the slicer attachment in position, separately slice the eggplant, squash, peppers, onion, and zucchini. Drain the diced tomatoes, reserving the liquid and 2 cups tomatoes.

2   Place reserved tomato liquid, basil, thyme, salt, pepper, sugar, water, tomato paste and garlic into the Ninja 40-oz. bowl with blade in position, and pulse for 10 seconds. Carefully remove blade.

3   Layer half the tomato paste mixture, the eggplant, yellow squash, 1 cup diced tomatoes, red pepper, onion, remaining diced tomatoes, the zucchini, and the remaining tomato paste mixture in a 9x13-inch baking dish. Cover the baking dish with parchment paper and aluminum foil.

4   Bake at 350° for 30 minutes. Remove the cover and continue to bake uncovered 40 minutes, or until vegetables are tender.

5   Remove from the oven and stir before serving.

TIP...

This versatile dish can be made in a sauté pan and combined with pasta to create a main dish for vegetarian friends and family. Serve with a good crusty bread to dip in it.

Mashed Cauliflower

Prep: 20 min. **Cook:** 12 min. **Serves:** 6
40-oz. bowl with blade attachment

A low-carb option for all the mashed potato lovers! With lots of flavor and a creamy texture, this recipe will give you a nice change of pace.—Stephen

Shopping List

1 head cauliflower, cut into florets

¼ cup whole milk

3 tablespoons unsalted butter

½ teaspoon salt

½ teaspoon ground black pepper

½ teaspoon ground coriander

3 ounces Parmesan cheese, cut into cubes

1 Pour 2 quarts of water into a 3-quart saucepan. Bring to a boil. Add cauliflower florets.

2 Cook 10 to 12 minutes or until fork-tender. Drain and set aside.

3 Place milk, butter, salt, pepper and coriander in a small saucepan.

4 Heat until butter is melted and mixture is warm.

5 Place cauliflower and Parmesan cheese into the Ninja 40-oz. bowl with blade in position. Pour milk mixture into the bowl and process for 10 to 15 seconds, or until all ingredients are fully combined. Carefully remove blade.

TIP...
To make it healthier, use fat-free milk and light butter. If you are a garlic fan, add ¼ teaspoon garlic powder.

Sweet Plantain Mash

Prep: 12 min. **Cook:** 1 hour **Serves:** 4
40-oz. bowl with blade attachment

Boiled, fried or baked, plantains are eaten every day in some countries. My favorite way to enjoy them made into a sweet and salty mash.—Andrea

Shopping List

3 ripe plantains, peeled

4 tablespoons unsalted butter, divided

1¼ cups half-and-half

⅓ cup packed light brown sugar

½ teaspoon each: salt and black pepper

1 Preheat oven to 350°. Cut 3 pieces of aluminum foil to wrap each plantain. Cut a ¼-inch deep slit in each plantain, lengthwise. Place ½ teaspoon butter into each slit. Use 1½ teaspoons of butter to butter each foil piece. Fully wrap, lightly, so steam can be created. Place seam-side-up on a jellyroll pan.

2 Bake at 350° for 1 hour. Remove from the oven and set aside.

3 Place the remaining butter, half-and-half, brown sugar, salt and pepper into a 1-quart saucepan.

4 Heat over medium heat until sugar is dissolved, stirring occasionally.

5 Cut plantains into 2½-inch pieces. Place into the Ninja 40-oz. bowl with blade in position. Pour half-and-half mixture into bowl and process for 20 seconds or until mixture is smooth. Carefully remove blade.

TIP...
The secret to this dish is really ripe plantains.

Desserts & Frozen Treats

Our favorite part of a meal—cakes, cupcakes, brownies and quick breads—go together so easily in your Ninja. Don't forget the frosting. Dulce de Leche Cream Cheese Frosting (page 140) and Quick and Easy Chocolate Ganache (page 140) finish desserts with a flourish.

The beauty of homemade ice creams is that you know what is in them, and the Ninja makes them almost instant. The use of frozen fruits as in Yogurt Fruit Ice Cream (page 149) creates a flawless texture. Be sure to check out the water ices, too.

A word from Bob...

Ice cream for one is a distinct possibility with the single-serve cup. About half the ingredients in our ice cream and water ice recipes in this chapter are made for one.

Vanilla Jellyroll

Prep: 30 min. **Cook:** 15 min. **Cool:** 45 min. **Serves:** 10
40-oz. bowl with dough blade attachment

Custom made to your liking, this basic Vanilla Jellyroll can be filled with any of the mousses, whipped creams, frostings and ganache recipes from this book.—Stephen

Shopping List

⅓ cup vegetable oil

½ cup water

1 (18¼-ounce) package yellow cake mix

1 teaspoon pure vanilla extract

4 large eggs

Confectioners' sugar

1 Preheat the oven to 350º. Lightly spray a 17x11x1-inch jellyroll pan with cooking spray. Line the pan with parchment paper to cover the bottom, and with a couple of inches extending at each end. Lightly spray with cooking spray.

2 Place oil, water, cake mix, vanilla and eggs into the Ninja 40-oz. bowl with blade in position, and pulse 5 times. Then process for 8 to 12 seconds or until well mixed. Carefully remove blade. Pour mixture evenly into prepared pan, smoothing it out with an offset spatula.

3 Bake for 15 to 18 minutes, or until a wooden pick inserted in the center comes out clean and the cake springs back when lightly touched.

4 Remove the cake from the oven and place on a cooling rack. Immediately dust a clean kitchen towel, larger than the size of the pan, with confectioners' sugar. Invert pan immediately onto the towel. Carefully peel the parchment paper. Roll the cake with the towel, while still hot, into a jellyroll. Place back on the cooling rack, seam side down, and let cool for no more than 45 minutes to prevent cracking.

5 Unroll the cake, fill with your favorite filling, then roll back into a jellyroll shape right away.

Vanilla Cheesecake

Prep: 20 min. **Cook:** 1 hour **Chill:** 6 hours **Serves:** 8
40-oz. bowl with blade attachment

This creamy and velvety cheesecake recipe is really light, but decadent. Serve plain or with your favorite toppings, like fruits, nuts, chocolate or caramel sauce.—Bob

Shopping List

1 package (9 or 10) graham crackers

⅓ cup plus ¾ cup sugar, divided

4 tablespoons (2 ounces) butter, melted

½ teaspoon cinnamon (optional)

2 (8-ounce) packages cream cheese, cut into 1-inch cubes, softened

½ cup sour cream

¾ cup heavy cream

2 tablespoons and 1 teaspoon all-purpose flour

2¼ teaspoons vanilla extract

3 large eggs

1 Preheat the oven to 350º.

2 Place graham crackers, roughly broken, into the Ninja 40-oz. bowl with blade in position, and pulse 8 to 10 times. Add ⅓ cup sugar, butter, and cinnamon, if using, and process until completely crumbled and well mixed. Carefully remove blade.

3 Press graham cracker mixture into the bottom of a 9-inch springform pan.

4 Bake for 8 minutes. Remove from the oven and let cool.

5 Place cream cheese, remaining ¾ cup sugar, sour cream, heavy cream, flour, vanilla and eggs into the 40-oz. bowl with blade in position, and pulse until mixture is thick and creamy. Carefully remove blade. Pour mixture into the cooled crust.

6 Bake for 50 to 60 minutes or until center is almost set (filling will be slightly soft).

7 Cool and refrigerate at least 6 hours or overnight before removing from pan.

TIP...

Use low-fat cream cheese and low-fat sour cream to make it a little healthier.

DESSERTS & FROZEN TREATS

Pumpkin Cupcakes

Prep: 8 min. **Cook:** 20 min. **Serves:** 24
40-oz. bowl with blade attachment

I don't like pumpkin pie or any other pumpkin dessert, for that matter. One day I mistakenly tried a spiced cupcake that turned out to be a moist, light and flavorful pumpkin cupcake. So here is my version.—Andrea

Shopping List

⅓ cup vegetable oil

½ cup whole milk

1 cup canned pumpkin purée

1 (18¼-ounce) package spice cake mix

3 large eggs

1 Preheat oven to 350°. Line 2 (12-cup) muffin pans with paper cupcake liners.

2 Place oil, milk, pumpkin purée, cake mix and eggs into the Ninja 40-oz. bowl with blade in position, and pulse 5 times. Then process for 10 seconds. Carefully remove blade. Divide mixture into prepared muffin pans, filling about ¾ full.

3 Bake for 20 to 22 minutes or until a wooden pick inserted in the center comes out clean.

TIP...

Top these delightful cupcakes with Cream Cheese Frosting (page 140) to make them even better.

Butterscotch Cupcakes

Prep: 8 min. **Cook:** 22 min. **Serves:** 16
40-oz. bowl with blade attachment

This cupcake was created to pair with the Dulce de Leche Cream Cheese Frosting recipe (page 141), which needed to have a perfect, light, caramel-flavored cupcake for it.—Andrea

Shopping List

½ cup vegetable oil

¼ cup whole milk

¾ cup water

1 teaspoon pure vanilla extract

1 (18¼-ounce) package yellow cake mix

1 (3.4-ounce) package butterscotch instant pudding mix

4 large eggs

1 Preheat oven to 350°. Line 2 (12-cup) muffin pans with paper cupcake liners.

2 Place oil, milk, water, vanilla, cake mix, pudding mix and eggs into the Ninja 40-oz. bowl with blade in position, and pulse 5 times. Then process for 10 seconds. Carefully remove blade.

3 Divide mixture into prepared muffin pans, filling about ¾ full.

4 Bake for 20 to 22 minutes or until a wooden pick inserted in the center comes out clean.

BUTTERSCOTCH CUPCAKES

137

Orange Yogurt Cupcakes

Prep: 8 min. **Cook:** 20 min. **Serves:** 24
40-oz. bowl with blade attachment

It's not really common to find orange-flavored cupcakes at your local bakery or supermarket. This quick and easy recipe will fulfill the craving.—Stephen

Shopping List

¾ cup orange juice

⅔ cup nonfat Greek yogurt

⅓ cup orange marmalade

⅓ cup vegetable oil

2 teaspoons grated orange zest

1 (18¼-ounce) package orange cake mix

4 large eggs

1 Preheat oven to 350°. Line 2 (12-cup) muffin pans with paper cupcake liners.

2 Place orange juice, yogurt, marmalade, oil, orange zest, cake mix and eggs into the Ninja 40-oz. bowl with blade in position, and pulse 5 times. Then process for 10 seconds. Carefully remove blade. Divide mixture into prepared muffin pans, filling about ¾ full.

3 Bake for 20 to 22 minutes or until a wooden pick inserted in the center comes out clean.

TIP...

Use store-bought orange juice not from concentrate. Substitute nonfat vanilla yogurt for nonfat Greek yogurt, if you wish.

Decadent Chocolate Cake

Prep: 8 min. **Cook:** 30 min. **Serves:** 8
40-oz. bowl with blade attachment

A quintessential American dessert, a chocolate cake has to be moist, chocolaty, rich, with a fine crumb that combines with a magnificent frosting to become the best dessert one could have.—Bob

Shopping List

Cocoa powder

½ cup vegetable oil

½ cup water

½ cup low-fat Greek yogurt

1 (18¼-ounce) package dark chocolate cake mix

1 (3.4-ounce) package butterscotch instant pudding mix

4 large eggs

1 cup whole milk

1 Preheat oven to 350°. Spray 2 (9-inch) cake pans with cooking spray and dust with cocoa powder.

2 Place oil, water, yogurt, cake mix, pudding mix, eggs and milk into the Ninja 40-oz. bowl with blade in position, and pulse 5 times. Then process for 10 to 15 seconds or until ingredients are well mixed. Carefully remove blade.

3 Pour mixture evenly into prepared pans.

4 Bake for 30 to 35 minutes or until a wooden pick inserted in the center comes out clean.

5 Cool cakes in pans on a cooling rack for 20 minutes. Invert cakes onto cooling rack and cool completely.

Carrot Cake

Prep: 20 min. **Cook:** 45 min. **Serves:** 10
40-oz. bowl with blade attachment

Very moist, and one of the best carrot cakes ever. It is loaded with carrots and cinnamon and sure to please any palate.—Bob

Shopping List

2 cups shredded carrots

½ cup chopped walnuts (optional)

½ cup vegetable oil

1 cup white sugar

1 teaspoon vanilla extract

1¼ cups all-purpose flour

1 teaspoon baking soda

1 teaspoon baking powder

¼ teaspoon salt

1¼ teaspoons ground cinnamon

2 large eggs

1 Preheat the oven to 350°. Spray an 8x4-inch (2-pound) loaf pan with cooking spray and dust with flour.

2 Place carrots and walnuts, if used, into a large mixing bowl. Set aside.

3 Add oil, sugar, vanilla, flour, baking soda, baking powder, salt, cinnamon and eggs Into the Ninja 40-oz. bowl with blade in position, and process for 15 to 20 seconds or until all ingredients are well mixed. Batter will be really thick. Carefully remove blade. Add batter to the mixing bowl with the carrots and nuts. Fold in all the ingredients with a spatula until well mixed. Pour the mixture into the prepared pan.

4 Bake for 45 to 55 minutes or until a wooden pick inserted into the center of the cake comes out clean. Let cool in pan for 20 minutes, then turn out onto a cooling rack and cool completely.

Cream Cheese Frosting

Prep: 5 min. **Yield:** 3 cups
40-oz. bowl with blade attachment

This is my all-time favorite frosting! It is great for Carrot Cake (page 139), Zucchini Bread (page 145) and with Pumpkin Cupcakes (page 136)—makes them taste even better.—Bob

Shopping List

2 (8-ounce) packages cream cheese, cut into 1-inch cubes and softened

1 (4-ounce) stick margarine, cut into 1-inch cubes and softened

1¾ cups confectioners' sugar

2 teaspoons pure vanilla extract

2 teaspoons fresh lime juice

1 Place cream cheese, margarine, sugar, vanilla and lime juice into the Ninja 40-oz. bowl with blade in position, and process for 15 seconds. Remove lid and carefully scrape down the sides of the bowl with a thin rubber spatula. Replace lid and pulse 8 to 10 times or until ingredients are well mixed and mixture is creamy.

2 Remove lid and carefully remove blade. Stir mixture with a spatula. Frost your cake right away, or refrigerate until needed. If refrigerated, let stand for 30 minutes before frosting your cakes.

TIP...

You can use lemon juice instead of lime juice, if you prefer.

Quick and Easy Chocolate Ganache

Prep: 4 min. **Stand:** 3 hours **Yield:** 2½ cups
40-oz. bowl with blade attachment

I love chocolate, and ganache is one of the most versatile recipes ever. You can eat it with a spoon right from the container, as a chocolate sauce when freshly made or as a cake or cupcake frosting when it has cooled.—Bob

Shopping List

1 pound (2½ cups) semisweet chocolate chips

1 cup plus 2 tablespoons evaporated milk

1 Place chocolate chips into a microwavable bowl and microwave for 1 minute. Stir until all the chocolate chips are completely melted. If necessary, microwave for 10 to 15 more seconds and stir again.

2 Pour evaporated milk into the Ninja 40-oz. bowl with blade in position. Pour in the chocolate and process for 25 seconds or until lightly thickened. Carefully remove blade.

3 Pour ganache into an airtight container and let stand at room temperature for 3 hours or overnight.

TIPS...

Store in the refrigerator for up to 2 weeks. Let stand at room temperature for 1 hour before using it.

For a little kick of extra flavor, stir 1½ teaspoons of instant granulated coffee into the melted chocolate chips right after it comes out of the microwave.

Dulce de Leche Cream Cheese Frosting

Prep: 5 min. **Yield:** 2 cups
40-oz. bowl with blade attachment

My two favorite toppings to eat with a cake or cupcake are Cream Cheese Frosting and Dulce de Leche. Marrying these two ingredients in the right proportions creates such a magical final product.—Andrea

Shopping List

2 (8-ounce) packages cream cheese, cut into 1-inch cubes and softened

7 ounces canned Dulce de Leche

1 Place cream cheese and Dulce de Leche, alternating them in layers, into the Ninja 40-oz. bowl with blade in position, and pulse 6 times. Then process for 10 seconds.

2 Remove lid and carefully scrape down the sides of the bowl with a thin rubber spatula. Replace lid and process for 5 to 10 more seconds. Carefully remove blade.

3 Cover the bowl and refrigerate until needed.

TIP...
This frosting is perfect for the Butterscotch Cupcakes (page 136) or the Vanilla Jellyroll (page 134).

Apricot Frosting

Prep: 5 min. **Yield:** 2½ cups
40-oz. bowl with blade attachment

A nice twist on a frosting that goes very well with chocolate, this is so fast to make that you will be finding new things to frost.—Stephen

Shopping List

2 ounces dried apricots

2 cups confectioners' sugar

2 tablespoons butter, softened

¼ cup plain Greek yogurt

1 Place apricots, sugar, butter and yogurt in the Ninja 40-oz. bowl with blade in position, and process for 10 seconds, or until well mixed and apricots are finely chopped.

2 Carefully remove blade and stir well.

TIP...
Experiment with other dried fruits in the same quantity for a whole world of variations.

Brownies

Prep: 15 min. **Cook:** 30 min. **Serves:** 9
40-oz. bowl with blade attachment

*This is the exact recipe that every gooey brownie lover should have
in their repertoire.—Andrea*

Shopping List

1¾ cups white sugar, divided

2 (4-ounce) sticks unsalted butter

3 ounces unsweetened chocolate, chopped

3 ounces semisweet chocolate chips

4 large eggs

1 teaspoon pure vanilla extract

1⅓ cups all-purpose flour

1 teaspoon salt

1 Preheat the oven to 350°.

2 Lightly spray a 9x9-inch baking pan with cooking spray.

3 Place 1 cup sugar, butter, chocolate and chocolate chips in a medium bowl
on top of a double boiler. Heat over medium-low heat until sugar dissolves,
stirring constantly. Set aside and cool for 10 minutes.

4 Add eggs, vanilla, remaining sugar, flour, salt and chocolate mixture into
the Ninja 40-oz. bowl with blade in position, and process for 20 seconds.
Remove lid and carefully scrape down sides of the bowl with a thin rubber
spatula. Replace lid and process for 5 more seconds. Carefully remove
blade. Pour batter into prepared pan.

5 Bake for 30 to 35 minutes or until brownies spring back when lightly touched.
Do not overbake.

6 Cool brownies in the pan on a cooling rack.

Raspberry Brownies

Prep: 10 min. **Cook:** 30 min. **Serves:** 9
40-oz. bowl with blade attachment

A simple swirl of warm seedless raspberry jam raises the bar for great brownie taste.—Bob

Shopping List

1 cup butter

1 (6-ounce) package semisweet chocolate chips

1 cup sugar

3 large eggs

1½ teaspoons vanilla extract

1¼ cups all-purpose flour

½ teaspoon salt

½ cup seedless raspberry jam

1 Preheat the oven to 350°. Spray a 13x9-inch baking dish with cooking spray.

2 Place butter and chocolate chips in a microwavable bowl and microwave for 1 minute; stir to melt. Cool to room temperature.

3 Place sugar, eggs, vanilla, chocolate mixture, flour and salt into the Ninja 40-oz. bowl with blade in position, and process for 10 seconds or until well mixed. Carefully remove blade. Pour chocolate mixture into prepared dish.

4 Place the jam in a microwavable bowl. Heat at HIGH for 15 seconds or until softened. Dollop the jam over the chocolate mixture and run a knife through to swirl the jam into the chocolate mixture.

5 Bake at 350° for 30 to 35 minutes or until center springs back when lightly touched. Cool before cutting.

Last Minute Brownies

Prep: 6 min. **Cook:** 35 min. **Serves:** 8
40-oz. bowl with blade attachment

These are the brownies to make when you have a dinner party or a gathering at a friend's house and forgot to make something ahead of time. Keep the brownie mixes and other ingredients on hand to be ready.—Bob

Shopping List

⅓ cup buttermilk

3 ounces vegetable oil

1 (18-ounce) package chocolate brownie mix

1 large egg

⅓ cup semisweet chocolate chips

1 Preheat the oven to 350°. Spray an 8x8-inch baking pan with cooking spray.

2 Place buttermilk, oil, brownie mix, egg and chocolate chips into the Ninja 40-oz. bowl with blade in position, and pulse 5 times. Then process for 15 seconds. Carefully remove blade. Pour mixture into prepared pan.

3 Bake for 35 to 45 minutes or until a wooden pick inserted in the center comes out clean.

TIP...
Add ½ cup chopped nuts before baking if you like nuts in your brownies.

Brownie Fig Bites

Prep: 5 min. **Serves:** 8
40-oz. bowl with blade attachment

Satisfy your chocolate craving with these deceptively easy no-cook confections.—Stephen

Shopping List

12 fig-filled cookies, broken into pieces

1 cup toasted pecans

2 tablespoons confectioner's sugar

1 (6-ounce) package semisweet chocolate chips, melted

1 Place cookies, pecans, sugar and chocolate in the Ninja 40-oz. bowl with blade in position, and process for 20 seconds or until well mixed. Carefully remove blade.

2 Spoon mixture by tablespoons and roll into walnut-sized balls.

TIP...
These confections may also be rolled in additional confectioners' sugar.

Zucchini Bread

Prep: 15 min. **Cook:** 35 min. **Serves:** 10
40-oz. bowl with blade attachment

This zucchini bread recipe is a great dessert for kids, so they will eat some vegetables without even knowing it.—Stephen

Shopping List

½ cup vegetable oil

1 cup white sugar

1½ teaspoons vanilla extract

1½ cups all-purpose flour

½ teaspoon each: salt, baking soda and baking powder

1½ teaspoons ground cinnamon

2 large eggs

2 cups shredded zucchini

1 Preheat the oven to 325°. Lightly spray an 8x4-inch nonstick loaf pan (2-pound loaf pan) with cooking spray.

2 Place oil, sugar, vanilla, flour, salt, baking soda, baking powder, cinnamon and eggs in the Ninja 40-oz. bowl with blade in position, and process for 15 to 20 seconds or until well mixed. The batter will be really thick. Carefully remove blade.

3 Place the zucchini in a mixing bowl. Add the flour mixture to the mixing bowl with the zucchini. Fold in all the ingredients until zucchini is fully incorporated. Pour the batter into the prepared pan.

4 Bake for 35 to 45 minutes, or until a wooden pick inserted in the center comes out clean. Let cool in pan for 20 minutes, then turn out onto a wire rack and cool completely.

Chocolate Chip Walnut Banana Bread

Prep: 6 min. **Cook:** 35 min. **Serves:** 10
40-oz. bowl with blade attachment

Banana bread is one of those quick breads that can come out really oily or really dry or sugary. Sometimes it is hard to find that happy medium. This recipe uses a store-bought mix and has been enhanced with fresh ingredients creating the perfect balance.—Bob

Shopping List

1 cup water

¼ cup vegetable oil

1 banana, peeled and cut in half

1 (14-ounce) package banana bread mix

¾ cup walnut halves

½ cup semisweet chocolate chips

2 large eggs

1 Preheat the oven to 350°. Lightly spray an 8x4-inch nonstick loaf pan (2-pound loaf pan) with cooking spray.

2 Place water, oil, banana, bread mix, walnuts, chocolate chips and eggs into the Ninja 40-oz. bowl with blade in position, and pulse 5 times. Then process for 15 seconds. Carefully remove blade. Pour mixture into prepared pan.

3 Bake for 35 to 45 minutes or until a wooden pick inserted in the center comes out clean.

Chocolate Rum Balls

Prep: 20 min. **Chill:** 2 hours **Serves:** 15
40-oz. bowl with blade attachment

*By far the easiest chocolate rum ball recipe ever made—
it is so rich and flavorful that there is never any left at
the end of the night.—Andrea*

Shopping List

1 pack crème-filled chocolate sandwich cookies

¾ cup evaporated milk

¼ cup rum

1 pound semisweet chocolate chips

1 Place cookies into the Ninja 40-oz. bowl with blade in position, and process until completely crumbled. Carefully remove blade. Pour crumbled cookies into a mixing bowl.

2 Pour evaporated milk and rum into the 40-oz. bowl with blade in position.

3 Place chocolate chips in a microwavable bowl and microwave for 1 minute. Stir until chocolate is evenly melted. If needed, microwave for 10 more seconds, and stir again. Pour melted chocolate into the Ninja 40-oz. bowl with the milk and rum, and process for 10 to 20 seconds or until slightly thickened and well mixed. Carefully remove blade.

4 Cover and refrigerate for 2 hours.

5 Shape mixture into ¾-inch balls and roll each ball in the crumbled cookies. Serve immediately or store in the refrigerator. Remove from the refrigerator half an hour before serving.

CHOCOLATE RUM BALLS

YOGURT FRUIT ICE CREAM

Yogurt Fruit Ice Cream

Prep: 5 min. **Serves:** 4
40-oz. bowl with blade attachment

Frozen yogurt has become so popular these days and is normally healthier than ice cream. You know exactly what's in your frozen treat with all-natural ingredients.—Bob

Shopping List

1½ cups nonfat Greek yogurt

⅓ cup granulated sugar substitute

10 to 12 ounces frozen sliced peaches, frozen whole strawberries, frozen blackberries, frozen mixed berries, frozen blueberries or frozen raspberries

1 Combine the yogurt and the sugar substitute and mix well.

2 Place the frozen fruit and the yogurt mixture alternately in layers, starting and ending with the frozen fruit, into the Ninja 40-oz. bowl with blade in position. Pulse 10 to 15 times or until fruit is broken down. Process for 35 to 45 seconds or until well mixed.

3 If a piece of fruit gets stuck on part of the blade, simply move it around with a spatula and mix for a couple more seconds or until well mixed. Carefully remove blade.

4 Serve ice cream with an ice cream scoop.

TIP...
You can substitute other fruits, such as: frozen bananas (12 ounces), frozen sliced mangoes (11 ounces) and frozen pineapple chunks (10 ounces).

Skinny Me Ice Cream

Prep: 5 min. **Serves:** 3
40-oz. bowl with blade attachment

Most of us try to watch our calories, fat and sugar intake. This ice cream is not only healthy and really delicious, but also fast and simple to make.—Andrea

Shopping List

¾ cup plus 3 tablespoons skim milk (7 ounces)

¼ cup granulated sugar substitute

9 to 11 ounces frozen sliced peaches, frozen whole strawberries, frozen blackberries, frozen mixed berries, frozen blueberries or frozen raspberries

1 Combine the skim milk and the sugar substitute and mix until the sugar substitute dissolves.

2 Place the frozen fruit into the Ninja 40-oz. bowl with blade in position. Add the milk mixture. Pulse 10 to 15 times or until fruit is broken up. Process for 20 to 25 seconds, pulsing from time to time, or until well mixed.

3 If a piece of fruit gets stuck on part of the blade, simply move it around with a spatula and mix for a couple more seconds or until well mixed. Carefully remove blade.

4 Serve ice cream with an ice cream scoop.

TIP...
Add a teaspoon of vanilla extract or ½ teaspoon of almond extract for a little extra flavor.

The Real Deal Fruit Ice Cream

Prep: 14 min. **Cook:** 8 min. **Serves:** 3
40-oz. bowl with blade attachment

Prepare this basic ice cream custard, then combine it with any one of the frozen fruit options provided to create your own homemade fruit ice cream.—Stephen

Shopping List for Custard Ice Cream Base (3 batches)

4 large eggs

½ cup sugar, divided

1½ teaspoons vanilla extract

1 cup heavy whipping cream

1 cup whole milk

1 Place the eggs, ¼ cup sugar and the vanilla in a medium bowl. Whisk until well mixed.

2 Pour the cream, milk and remaining sugar into a medium saucepan. Heat over medium heat to just under a boil, stirring occasionally. Slowly add the cream mixture to the egg mixture, stirring constantly so the eggs don't cook.

3 Pour the mixture through a mesh strainer into a metal bowl and refrigerate immediately. When the mixture is cooled, measure 9 ounces of the custard into individual containers and refrigerate until needed.

Shopping List for Ice Cream (Serves 3)

9 to 12 ounces frozen sliced peaches, frozen whole strawberries, frozen blackberries, frozen mixed berries, frozen blueberries or frozen raspberries

1 cup Custard Ice Cream Base

1 Place the frozen fruit into the Ninja 40-oz. bowl with blade in position. Pour the custard mixture over the fruit. Pulse 10 to 15 times or until fruit is broken up. Process for 30 seconds, pulsing once in a while until well mixed.

2 If a piece of fruit gets stuck on part of the blade, simply move it around with a spatula and process for a couple more seconds until well mixed. Carefully remove the blade.

3 Serve ice cream with an ice cream scoop.

TIP...
You can double the recipe for the custard and keep it stored in an airtight container in the refrigerator for up to 2 weeks.

Instant No-Fuss Ice Cream

Prep: 4 min. **Serves:** 2
40-oz. bowl with blade attachment

One of the most convenient ice creams to make, use the milk and sugar already in the house. If you keep some frozen fruit on-hand, you can make it any time.—Bob

Shopping List

1 cup whole milk

2 tablespoons sugar

10 to 11 ounces frozen sliced peaches, frozen whole strawberries, frozen blackberries, frozen mixed berries, frozen blueberries or frozen raspberries

1 Combine the milk and the sugar in a small bowl. Stir until the sugar dissolves.

2 Place the frozen fruit into the Ninja 40-oz. bowl with blade in position. Pour in the milk mixture and pulse 10 to 15 times or until fruit is broken up. Process for 20 to 25 seconds, pulsing from time to time, or until well mixed.

3 If a piece of fruit gets stuck on part of the blade, simply move it around with a spatula and pulse for a couple more seconds or until well mixed. Carefully remove blade.

4 Serve ice cream with an ice cream scoop.

TIP...
Substitute frozen bananas for the frozen fruit for some extra flavor and a little extra potassium.

Pineapple Coconut Water Ice

Prep: 10 min. **Serves:** 6
40-oz. bowl with blade attachment

A traditional Italian treat created with tropical flavors, this makes for a great afternoon snack to enjoy at home and feel like you are at the beach.—Bob

Shopping List

¼ pineapple, peeled, cored and cut into 1-inch cubes

1 (17-ounce) bottle coconut water

2 tablespoons sugar

1 lime, peeled, cut in half

1 Place pineapple, coconut water, sugar and lime in the Ninja 40-oz. bowl with blade in position, and process for 30 seconds. Carefully remove blade.

2 Pour mixture into ice cube trays and freeze for 5 to 6 hours or until frozen completely solid.

3 When frozen, place ice cubes in 2 batches in the 40-oz. bowl with blade in position, and process for 15 seconds each. Carefully remove blade.

TIP...
For a creamier water ice, use 1½ cups coconut water and ½ cup unsweetened coconut milk. Use frozen pineapple chunks, thawed, if you don't want to peel and cut your own.

Cherry Water Ice

Prep: 10 min. **Serves:** 6
40-oz. bowl with blade attachment

A mixture of dark sweet cherries and apricot nectar makes a delicious, melt-in-your-mouth frozen treat. Nectars are thicker and richer than regular juices and create a much "creamier" water ice.—Stephen

Shopping List

12 ounces dark sweet cherries

16 ounces apricot nectar

1 Place cherries and nectar in the Ninja 40-oz. bowl with blade in position, and process for 30 to 35 seconds or until well mixed. Carefully remove blade.

2 Pour liquid into ice cube trays and freeze for 5 to 6 hours or until frozen completely solid.

3 When frozen, place ice cubes in 2 batches in the 40-oz. bowl with blade in position, and process for 15 seconds each. Carefully remove blade.

TIP...
You don't have to blend in a fruit. Just freeze any nectar into ice cubes. When frozen solid, process 7 ice cubes per batch in a Ninja 16-oz. chopper bowl with blade in position for 10 to 15 seconds or until well mixed.

Lemon Water Ice

Prep: 8 min. **Serves:** 4
40-oz. bowl with blade attachment

Water ice, also known as Italian ice, is a sweetened frozen dessert made with fruit concentrates, juices, purées or other food flavorings. Here is our all-natural version of the bestselling traditional flavor.—Stephen

Shopping List

2 lemons, peeled, cut into quarters

13½ ounces lemonade

2 tablespoons honey

1 Place lemons, lemonade and honey in the Ninja 40-oz. bowl with blade in position, and process for 30 seconds. Carefully remove blade.

2 Strain mixture into a bowl. Discard pulp.

3 Pour liquid into ice cube trays and freeze 5 to 6 hours until frozen completely solid.

4 When frozen, place ice cubes in 2 batches in the 40-oz. bowl with blade in position, and process for 15 seconds each. Carefully remove blade.

TIP...
This treat is really tart so add an extra tablespoon of honey to the mixture before freezing into ice cubes if you like it a little less tart.

LEMON WATER ICE

CHOCOLATE BANANA
PEANUT BUTTER ICE CREAM

Chocolate Banana Peanut Butter Ice Cream

Prep: 14 min. **Serves:** 4
40-oz. bowl with blade attachment

The traditional combination of peanut butter and chocolate adds an extra added treat—bananas—to make it sweeter and more decadent. Make the chocolate milk ice cubes the day before so they are ready when you need them.—Stephen

Shopping List

12 chocolate milk ice cubes (use only reduced-fat [2%] or low-fat [1%] chocolate milk)

1 banana, peeled, cut into ½-inch slices and frozen

1 tablespoon creamy peanut butter

¼ cup chocolate syrup

1 To make the chocolate milk ice cubes, pour the chocolate milk into ice cube trays and freeze 6 hours or overnight, until frozen completely solid.

2 Place the frozen chocolate milk ice cubes and the frozen banana pieces, alternating them, into the Ninja 40-oz. bowl with blade in position. Add the peanut butter and the chocolate syrup.

3 Pulse 15 to 20 times or until the fruit is broken up. Process for 30 to 40 seconds, pulsing from time to time, or until well mixed.

4 If a piece of fruit gets stuck on part of the blade, simply move it around with a spatula and process for a couple more seconds or until well mixed. Carefully remove the blade.

5 Serve the ice cream with an ice cream scoop.

STRAWBERRY JAM   P 158

Go-Withs

The little extra touches are what makes cooking so much fun. Try Onion Jam (page 163) or Mediterranean Butter (page 158) with your next grilled meats, and sit back and wait for the praise and rave reviews.

Homemade is miles better than store-bought, as you will see when you make French Onion Dip (page 166), your own Hummus (page 177) or Olive Tapenade (page 172).

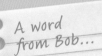

A word from Bob...

Time is such a precious thing for each of us. Your Ninja and our recipes will save a lot of it for you. And you will be creating family favorites at the same time.

Included in this chapter...

Strawberry Jam

Prep: 5 min. **Cook:** 35 min.
Cool: 15 min. **Yield:** 3 cups
40 oz. bowl with blade attachment

I absolutely love strawberry jam especially with waffles, toast, muffins, pancakes and croissants. After making my own homemade version, I have never bought a single jar at the supermarket again.—Andrea

Shopping List

1½ pounds strawberries, stems cut off and cut in half, divided

2 cups white sugar

¼ cup lemon juice

1 Place half of strawberries into the Ninja 40-oz. bowl with blade in position. Pulse 10 times or until roughly chopped. Carefully remove blade and strawberries. Repeat with the remaining strawberries.

2 Place all the strawberries, sugar and lemon juice into a medium-size saucepan and stir until well mixed.

3 Cook over high heat and bring to a boil. Reduce heat to medium low and cook for 35 to 45 minutes or until lightly thickened, stirring frequently.

4 Remove from heat and cool for 15 minutes. Pour the mixture into a glass or plastic container, cover and refrigerate.

TIP...
Use this basic recipe to make raspberry, blackberry or blueberry jam by substituting those berries for the strawberries.

Mediterranean Butter

Prep: 15 min. **Chill:** 1 hour **Yield:** 2 cups
40-oz. bowl with blade attachment

Traditional steak houses place a couple pats of seasoned butter on your steak to enhance the flavor. You can also serve this complex version with fish and chicken.—Stephen

Shopping List

1 red bell pepper, roasted, cut into quarters

¾ cup sun-dried tomatoes packed in oil, drained

½ cup fresh basil leaves

2 cloves garlic, peeled

1 teaspoon capers, drained

3 (4-ounce) sticks unsalted butter, softened

½ teaspoon ground black pepper

½ teaspoon salt

1 Place red pepper, tomatoes, basil, garlic, capers, butter, black pepper and salt into the Ninja 40-oz. bowl with blade in position, and process for 25 seconds. Carefully remove blade.

2 Place the mixture on a large piece of plastic wrap and roll into a log shape.

3 Wrap and refrigerate until firm, about 1 hour.

TIP...
If you are watching your cholesterol, you can substitute extra virgin olive oil for the butter. Keep the mixture refrigerated. Drizzle on your meat.

Praline Butter

Prep: 15 min. **Chill:** 1 hour **Yield:** 2 cups
40-oz. bowl with blade attachment

Early pralines in France were whole almonds individually coated in caramelized sugar, brought to Louisiana by French settlers. They are the inspiration for this compound butter to spread on toast or waffles.—Bob

Shopping List

3 (4-ounce) sticks unsalted butter, softened

6 ounces pecan halves, toasted

1½ teaspoons ground cinnamon

¾ cup caramel sauce

1. Place butter, pecans, cinnamon and caramel sauce into the Ninja 40-oz. bowl with blade in position, and process for 20 seconds. Carefully remove blade.
2. Place the mixture on a large piece of plastic wrap and roll into a log shape.
3. Wrap and refrigerate until it hardens, about 1 hour.

Apple Compote

Prep: 10 min. **Cook: 9 min.** **Yield:** 1½ cups
40-oz. bowl with slicer attachment

Apples pair with many dishes—atop pancakes, pork chops, baked Brie cheese, or even cheesecake. You can add a little spice and fresh herbs to balance the sweetness.—Bob

Shopping List

2 Granny Smith apples, peeled and cored

2 tablespoons unsalted butter

⅓ cup dark raisins

2 tablespoons light brown sugar

¼ teaspoon vanilla extract

⅛ teaspoon ground cinnamon

⅛ teaspoon ground nutmeg

1. Slice the apples in the Ninja 40-oz. bowl with the slicer attachment in position.
2. Heat the butter in a large sauté pan over medium-high heat. Stir in the apples, raisins, brown sugar, vanilla, cinnamon and nutmeg. Cover the pan.
3. Cook for 5 minutes. Remove the lid and cook uncovered for an additional 4 minutes, stirring occasionally.

TIP...

For savory dishes, add 4 large leaves of basil, ¼ teaspoon ground ginger, ¼ teaspoon ground black pepper and 1 teaspoon apple cider vinegar while cooking.

Chocolate Mousse

Prep: 14 min. **Yield:** 1½ cups
16-oz. chopper bowl with blade attachment or single-serve cup

Everyone's favorite topping or dessert is sometimes hard to make. This basic simple recipe uses our ganache recipe to make it even more decadent.—Stephen

Shopping List

1 cup cold heavy whipping cream

5 tablespoons Quick and Easy Chocolate Ganache (page 140), or 4 tablespoons chocolate fudge sauce

1 Place heavy cream into the Ninja 16-oz. bowl with blade in position. Add the ganache.

2 Process for 15 to 20 seconds until medium peaks form. Carefully remove blade.

3 Serve immediately or store in the refrigerator.

TIP...

When making any whipped cream or mousse, it always helps to chill the container you are using to whip the heavy cream.

Instant Fruit Whipped Cream

Prep: 3 min. **Yield:** 12 ounces
16-oz. single-serve cup or chopper bowl with blade attachment

I didn't have the fruit needed for the whipped cream topping I was making for dessert so I came up with a simple fruit-flavored whipped cream topping, using jam to replace the sugar and fruit.—Andrea

Shopping List

1 cup cold heavy whipping cream

3 tablespoons of your favorite jam, marmalade or preserves

1 Place heavy cream and jam into the Ninja 16-oz. chopper bowl with blade in position.

2 Process for 10 to 15 seconds or until medium peaks form. Carefully remove blade.

3 Serve or store in the refrigerator.

No-Fuss Whipped Cream

Prep: 2 min. **Yield:** 1½ cups
16-oz. single-serve cup or chopper bowl with blade attachment

As easy as 1, 2, 3, this recipe is quick with no chemicals, preservatives or fake oils. Your homemade version will be your new favorite to garnish all your sweet dishes for your family and friends.—Stephen

Shopping List

1¼ cups cold heavy whipping cream

¼ cup confectioners' sugar

1 teaspoon pure vanilla extract

1 Place the heavy cream into the Ninja 16-oz. cup.

2 Add the sugar and vanilla. Screw on the blade cap.

3 Process for 8 to 10 seconds or until medium peaks form.

4 Serve immediately or store in the refrigerator.

TIP...

For a little twist, substitute ½ teaspoon almond extract for the vanilla. For the Ninja 40-oz. bowl, make 2½ times the recipe.

Dulce de Leche Mousse

Prep: 4 min. **Yield:** 1½ cups
16-oz. chopper bowl or single-serve cup

Dulce de leche is widely used in Latin America not only as the main component of a dessert but also as an accompaniment or topping for it. This recipe gives you the flavor of dulce de leche to top your favorite desserts without being overly sweet.—Andrea

Shopping List

1 cup cold heavy whipping cream

4 tablespoons canned dulce de leche

1 Place heavy cream into the Ninja 16-oz. cup then add the dulce de leche.

2 Process for 15 to 20 seconds or until medium peaks form.

3 Serve or store in the refrigerator.

TIP...

You can find canned dulce de leche in most supermarkets, next to the condensed milk section or in any Latin food store.

Mango Chutney

Prep: 10 min. **Cook:** 19 min. **Yield:** 1½ cups
16-oz. chopper bowl with blade attachment

Chutneys are made from many combinations of fruits and vegetables and can be served hot or sweet. In the United States, fruit, vinegar and sugar are the key ingredients.—Bob

Shopping List

1¾ ounces shallot, peeled

¼ ounce fresh ginger, peeled

1 teaspoon vegetable oil

9 ounces peeled and seeded mango

½ cup fresh parsley leaves

¾ cup golden raisins

2 tablespoons lime juice

1 tablespoon honey

1 teaspoon apple cider vinegar

¼ teaspoon salt

¼ teaspoon ground black pepper

¼ teaspoon crushed red pepper flakes

¼ teaspoon turmeric

⅛ teaspoon ground nutmeg

1 Place the shallot and ginger in the Ninja 16-oz. chopper bowl with blade in position, and pulse 6 times. Carefully remove blade.

2 Heat the oil in a medium saucepan over medium-high heat. Add the ginger and shallot.

3 Cook for 4 minutes, stirring occasionally, or until shallot and ginger are tender.

4 Place the mango and parsley in the Ninja 16-oz. chopper bowl with blade in position, and pulse 6 times. Carefully remove blade.

5 Add the mango mixture, raisins, lime juice, honey, vinegar, salt, pepper, red pepper flakes, turmeric and nutmeg to the saucepan.

6 Cook for 15 minutes over medium heat, stirring occasionally.

7 Cool and refrigerate.

Quick and Easy Kim Chee

Prep: 2 hours **Yield:** 20 ounces
40-oz. bowl with slicer attachment and 16-oz. chopper bowl

Originally placed in clay pots and buried for thirty days to ferment, this Korean dish is a staple of Korean food. You can enjoy this quick version the following day.—Stephen

Shopping List

10 ounces Napa cabbage

2 teaspoons salt

3 cups cold water

2 tablespoons sugar

¼ cup red pepper paste

1 clove garlic, peeled

½ ounce fresh ginger, peeled

½ cup rice wine vinegar

¾ cup sliced green onions

1 Slice the cabbage in the Ninja 40-oz. bowl with the slicer attachment in position.

2 Place the sliced cabbage in a bowl and stir in the salt and water until well mixed. Let sit for 2 hours. Drain.

3 Place the sugar, red pepper paste, garlic, ginger, vinegar and green onions in the Ninja 16-oz. chopper bowl with blade in position, and purée until well mixed. Carefully remove blade and pour over cabbage mixture; mix well.

4 Place in a sealed container and refrigerate overnight.

TIP...

If you can't find red pepper paste, substitute dried chiles reconstituted in water.

Onion Jam

Prep: 10 min. **Cook:** 30 min. **Cool:** 30 min.
Yield: 2 cups
40-oz. bowl with blade attachment

The diversity of this condiment is endless. Serve it with a steak, chicken breast, fillet of fish or lamb, on a crescent roll, with asparagus, on a crostini bread or burger or any other way you can find.—Bob

Shopping List

1 tablespoon vegetable oil

2 medium onions, sliced

¼ cup red wine vinegar

2 tablespoons light brown sugar

1 teaspoon ground black pepper

½ teaspoon salt

1 teaspoon dried thyme

1 cup red wine

1 Heat the oil in a large sauté pan over medium-high heat. Add the onions.

2 Cook 10 minutes, stirring occasionally. Reduce heat to medium. Stir in vinegar, brown sugar, pepper, salt, thyme and wine.

3 Cook 20 minutes, stirring occasionally. Cool.

4 Pour onion mixture into the Ninja 40-oz. bowl with blade in position, and process for 20 seconds. Carefully remove blade.

TIP...

Whenever you serve this jam, try adding goat cheese for a perfect pairing.

Hot Pepper Relish

Prep: 20 min. **Cook:** 25 min. **Yield:** 16 ounces
40-oz. bowl with blade attachment or 16-oz. chopper bowl

When I host a cookout, I always have a nice spread of homemade condiments whether to top a burger, hot dog, chicken, steak or a piece of fish. This relish has a perfect balance to complement anything you make.—Andrea

Shopping List

1 red bell pepper, cored

1 green bell pepper, cored

1 jalapeño pepper

½ medium yellow onion, peeled

2 cloves garlic, peeled

1 teaspoon dried thyme

⅛ teaspoon ground cinnamon

¼ teaspoon ground allspice

2 tablespoons light brown sugar

2 tablespoons apple cider vinegar

2 tablespoons Dijon mustard

½ teaspoon ground black pepper

¼ teaspoon salt

3 dill pickle spears

1 cup fresh parsley leaves

¼ cup dill pickle juice

1 Place the red and green peppers, jalapeño, onion and garlic in the Ninja 40-oz. bowl with blade in position, and process for 10 seconds. Carefully remove blade.

2 Place the pepper mixture, thyme, cinnamon, allspice, brown sugar, vinegar, mustard, pepper and salt into a medium saucepan.

3 Cook over medium heat for 25 minutes. Remove from the heat and cool.

4 Place the pickle spears, parsley and pickle juice in the Ninja 16-oz. chopper bowl, and process for 10 seconds. Carefully remove blade. Stir the pickle mixture into the cooled pepper mixture.

5 Refrigerate.

French Onion Dip

Prep: 15 min. **Cook:** 20 min.
Cool: 1 hour **Yield:** 5 cups
40-oz. bowl with blade attachment

Everyone at work could not stop eating this onion dip and it disappeared so fast. What a difference between homemade and one bought in the store!—Stephen

Shopping List

1 tablespoon vegetable oil

3 medium yellow onions, sliced

⅓ cup malt vinegar

1 (8-ounce) package cream cheese, softened

1 cup sour cream

1 (1-ounce) package ranch dip mix

1 Heat the oil In a 3-quart saucepan. Add the onions.

2 Cook over medium-high heat until the onions are tender and caramelized (medium brown in color). Add the vinegar and stir to mix well. Set aside and cool completely.

3 Place the cream cheese, sour cream, ranch dip mix and cooled onions in the Ninja 40-oz. bowl with blade in position, and process for 30 seconds. Carefully remove blade.

4 Refrigerate the onion dip for 1 hour prior to serving, allowing the flavors to blend.

TIP...
Add 3 tablespoons of horseradish to give it a little kick.

Buffalo Chicken Wing Dip

Prep: 18 min. **Cook:** 30 min. **Yield:** 4½ cups
40-oz. bowl with blade attachment

This dip tastes just like I am eating chicken wings with blue cheese sauce, hanging out at my favorite bar with my friends watching sports on the big screen.—Stephen

Shopping List

6 ounces precooked chicken strips

2 (8-ounce) packages cream cheese, softened

½ cup ranch dressing

½ cup blue cheese dressing

¾ cup Buffalo wing sauce or hot sauce

1 cup shredded Colby Monterey Jack cheese, divided

1 Preheat oven to 350°.

2 Place chicken, cream cheese, ranch dressing, blue cheese dressing, sauce and half of the shredded Colby Monterey Jack cheese into the Ninja 40-oz. bowl with blade in position.

3 Process for 15 to 20 seconds or until creamy and well mixed. Carefully remove blade. Pour the mixture into an 8x8-inch pan and sprinkle the remaining cheese on top.

4 Bake for 30 minutes. Let the dip cool for 10 minutes before serving.

TIP...
To spice it up a bit more, drizzle some extra buffalo wing sauce on top before serving.

Crab Dip

Prep: 10 min. **Yield:** 3 cups
40-oz. bowl with blade attachment

My chef friend in Maryland had a pile of fresh cooked crabs. This great dip was the happy result from the broken lumps his cooks left behind when picking the meat from the crabs.—Andrea

Shopping List

1 (8-ounce) package cream cheese, softened

8 ounces lump crabmeat

¾ cup mayonnaise

9 dashes hot sauce

2 teaspoons Dijon mustard

1 teaspoon Worcestershire sauce

2 tablespoons freshly squeezed lemon juice

½ red bell pepper, roasted, cut into ½-inch pieces

1 green onion, cut into 5 pieces

1 Place the cream cheese, crabmeat, mayonnaise, hot sauce, mustard, Worcestershire, lemon juice, red pepper and onion into the Ninja 40-oz. bowl with blade in position.

2 Process for 20 seconds. Carefully remove blade.

TIP...
Always pick over the crab to be sure to avoid any pieces of shell in your dip.

Italian White Bean Dip

Prep: 20 min. **Yield:** 4 cups
40-oz. bowl with blade attachment

In Italy I enjoyed a very delicious treat served as an antipasto. It was flavorful and light. I was able to duplicate it here for you— enjoy!—Andrea

Shopping List

2 (15-ounce) cans cannellini beans, drained and rinsed

4 tablespoons freshly squeezed lemon juice

⅓ cup extra virgin olive oil

3 cloves garlic, peeled

4 marinated sun-dried tomatoes

½ red bell pepper, roasted, cut into 1-inch pieces

1½ teaspoons onion powder

1 teaspoon dried parsley flakes

½ teaspoon salt

¾ teaspoon ground black pepper

1 tablespoon chopped fresh parsley

1 Place beans, lemon juice, oil, garlic, tomatoes, red pepper, onion powder, dried parsley, salt and black pepper into the Ninja 40-oz. bowl with blade in position.

2 Pulse 10 times then process until creamy. Carefully remove blade.

3 Sprinkle with parsley before serving.

TIP...
You can use garbanzo beans or even red kidney beans instead of cannellini.

Spinach Artichoke Dip

Prep: 14 min. **Cook:** 25 min. **Yield:** 5 cups
40-oz. bowl with blade attachment

This very popular dip is everywhere! Enjoy this version with a secret ingredient—white wine.—Bob

Shopping List

2 (8-ounce) packages cream cheese, softened

1 (13¾-ounce) can artichoke hearts, drained, reserve ⅓ cup of the liquid

1 (10-ounce) package frozen spinach, thawed, well drained

1 (5-ounce) wedge Parmesan cheese, cut into half-inch cubes

1 teaspoon garlic powder

Salt and ground black pepper to taste

⅓ cup white wine

¼ cup grated Parmesan cheese

1 Preheat oven to 350°.

2 Place cream cheese, artichoke hearts, spinach, cheese cubes, garlic powder, salt, pepper and wine into the Ninja 40-oz. bowl with blade in position.

3 Pulse 15 times or until the mixture is creamy. Carefully remove blade.

4 Pour the mixture into an 8x8-inch baking pan. Sprinkle grated Parmesan cheese on top.

5 Bake for 25 to 30 minutes or until heated through.

TIP...

I normally bake it in a round bread loaf. Cut ¼ of the top off, scoop out the bread and fill with the dip. Bake as above.

SPINACH ARTICHOKE DIP

Taco Dip

Prep: 15 min. **Cook:** 12 min. **Yield:** 5 cups
40-oz. bowl with blade attachment

This quick and easy dip has all the flavors that Mexican food has to offer in just one dish. Serve with tortilla chips. Use chicken breast instead of beef for a healthier version.—Bob

Shopping List

1 pound lean beef chuck roast, cut into 1-inch cubes

2 teaspoons olive oil

1 (1-ounce) package hot and spicy taco seasoning

1 cup sour cream

1 (10-ounce) can diced tomatoes with green chiles, drained

2 green onions, cut into 1-inch pieces

¾ cup dark red kidney beans, drained and rinsed

1 (15-ounce) can black olives, drained

¼ cup chili sauce

1 cup shredded Cheddar cheese

1 Place the beef into the Ninja 40-oz. bowl with blade in position, and process until finely ground. Carefully remove blade.

2 Pour the olive oil Into a 3-quart sauce-pan and heat over medium heat. When the oil is hot, add the ground beef.

3 Cook the beef for 8 minutes or until it is no longer pink, stirring frequently to break up meat. Reduce heat to low and stir in the taco seasoning. Cook for 4 more minutes, stirring occasionally. Remove from heat and set aside.

4 Place the sour cream, tomatoes with chiles, onions, beans, olives and chili sauce into the Ninja 40-oz. bowl with blade in position, and process for 10 seconds or until the mixture is well mixed but still chunky. Carefully remove blade.

5 Pour the sour cream mixture over the cooked beef and mix well. Add the cheese and stir until well mixed.

A word from Bob...

A great way to serve this dip for a party is to portion it out in small cups so everyone has his or her own personal serving with chips and no messy serving dish!

TIP...

For a hot dip, pour the mixture into an 8x8-inch baking pan. Top with an extra ½ cup shredded cheese and bake at 350° for 30 minutes.

Pizza Dip

Prep: 20 min. **Cook:** 20 min. **Yield:** 5 cups
40-oz. bowl with blade attachment

A dip that has all the taste of a pizza! I serve this when I entertain. Just serve with crackers or any bread cut into bite-size pieces.—Stephen

Shopping List

½ green bell pepper, seeded and cut into 2-inch pieces

¼ red onion, peeled and cut in half

15 large black olives

4 ounces whole pepperoni stick, cut into ½-inch circles

1½ teaspoons ground black pepper

1 tablespoon Italian seasoning

8 ounces mozzarella cheese, cut into ½-inch cubes

1 (8-ounce) package cream cheese

1 (15-ounce) can pizza sauce

1 teaspoon crushed red pepper

½ cup shredded mozzarella cheese

1 Preheat oven to 350°.

2 Place the bell pepper, onion, olives, pepperoni, black pepper, seasoning and mozzarella cheese into the Ninja 40-oz. bowl with blade in position, and pulse 15 times. Remove the lid. Add the cream cheese, pizza sauce and red pepper, and process for 35 seconds. Carefully remove blade.

3 Pour the mixture into an 8x8-inch baking pan and spread evenly. Sprinkle the shredded mozzarella on top.

4 Bake for 20 minutes or until heated through.

Smoked Salmon Spread

Prep: 15 min. **Yield:** 5 cups
40-oz. bowl with blade attachment

Either a brunch idea or party pleaser, smoked salmon is always a hit. I love eating this spread for breakfast on a toasted pumpernickel bagel or as a snack with some crackers. Indulge yourself and make it for more than special occasions.—Bob

Shopping List

1 (8-ounce) package cream cheese, cut in cubes, softened

8 ounces sliced smoked salmon, cut in pieces

2 teaspoons capers, drained

¼ cup loosely packed fresh dill

⅓ cup sour cream

¼ small shallot, peeled and cut in half

1 teaspoon ground black pepper

¼ cup buttermilk

1 Place cream cheese, salmon, capers, dill, sour cream, shallot, pepper and buttermilk into the Ninja 40-oz. bowl with blade in position.

2 Process for 20 seconds. Carefully remove blade.

TIP...
Serve this delicious spread atop an onion bagel with sliced tomato and cornichons or simply with pita bread.

Olive Tapenade

Prep: 18 min. **Yield:** 1⅓ cups
16-oz. chopper bowl with blade attachment

Popular in the south of France, this dish gets its name from the Provençal word for capers and usually has anchovies in it. I created this recipe without them.—Andrea

Shopping List

¼ cup marinated sun-dried tomatoes

½ red pepper, roasted, cut into chunks

2 sprigs flat leaf parsley

6 basil leaves

½ teaspoon capers, drained

1 cup large black olives

⅓ cup pimento-stuffed green olives

1 teaspoon lemon juice

1 tablespoon extra virgin olive oil

2 cloves garlic, peeled

½ teaspoon ground black pepper

1 Place tomatoes, red pepper, parsley, basil, capers, olives, lemon juice, oil, garlic and black pepper into the Ninja 16-oz. chopper bowl with blade in position.

2 Pulse 5 to 7 times or until roughly chopped. Carefully remove blade.

TIP...
Make one day ahead and refrigerate. For the 40-oz. bowl, double the recipe.

Bruschetta

Prep: 10 min. **Yield:** 1¼ cups
16-oz. chopper bowl with blade attachment

Bruschetta is an antipasto from Italy consisting of toasted bread rubbed with garlic and topped with extra virgin olive oil, salt and pepper. I love to top my bruschetta with this topping recipe.—Stephen

Shopping List

2 tomatoes, cut into quarters

¼ cup marinated sun-dried tomatoes

6 basil leaves

2 cloves garlic, peeled

1 tablespoon extra virgin olive oil

1 teaspoon balsamic vinegar

¼ teaspoon salt

¼ teaspoon ground black pepper

1 Place tomatoes, basil, garlic, oil, vinegar, salt and pepper into the Ninja 16-oz. chopper bowl with blade in position.

2 Pulse 5 to 7 times or until roughly chopped. Carefully remove blade.

TIP...
Whenever possible I buy fresh mozzarella di bufalo that I slice and put between the bread and the topping for a fantastic bruschetta. For the 40-oz. bowl, double the recipe.

Mango Salsa

Prep: 20 min. **Yield:** 1¼ cups
16-oz. chopper bowl with blade attachment

Next time you have a Latin-themed dinner, make this salsa instead of the more traditional ones. It's so light and refreshing and goes great with chips . . . but also on top of your salad or tacos.—Bob

Shopping List

1 ripe mango, peeled, pitted and cut into chunks

⅛ medium red onion, peeled

¼ cup loosely packed fresh cilantro leaves

½ jalapeño pepper, top cut off, seeded and cut in half

⅛ teaspoon ground black pepper

¼ teaspoon salt

1 teaspoon honey

2 teaspoons lime juice

1   Place mango, onion, cilantro, jalapeño, black pepper, salt, honey and lime juice into the Ninja 16-oz. chopper bowl with blade in position.

2   Pulse 5 to 6 times or until chopped as desired. Carefully remove blade.

TIP...
If you like papaya, you can use it instead of mango. Lemon juice works as well as lime juice. For the Ninja 40-oz. bowl, double the recipe.

Tomato Salsa

Prep: 14 min. **Yield:** 1 cup
16-oz. chopper bowl with blade attachment

Every really traditional Latin restaurant will have a tomato salsa as a condiment to be eaten with chips, burritos or tacos, or on top of carnitas or barbacoa. You could call it "the Latin Ketchup."—Andrea

Shopping List

⅛ red onion, peeled and cut in half

¼ cup loosely packed cilantro

½ jalapeño pepper, top cut off, seeded and cut into chunks

2 vine-ripe tomatoes, tops cut off and quartered

⅛ teaspoon ground black pepper

¼ teaspoon salt

2 tablespoons fresh lime juice

1   Place onion, cilantro, jalapeño, tomatoes, black pepper, salt and lime juice into the Ninja 16-oz. chopper bowl with blade in position.

2   Pulse 5 to 7 times or until chopped as desired. Carefully remove blade.

TIP...
Mix with a can of black beans or a cup of cooked corn kernels to create a different version. For the 40-oz. bowl, double the recipe.

PINEAPPLE SALSA

Pineapple Salsa

Prep: 25 min. **Yield:** 1¼ cups
16-oz. chopper bowl with blade attachment

I had the pleasure of trying a pineapple salsa while vacationing in Jamaica. It was served as a dip with chips, but also on a grilled piece of blackened grouper for dinner. Fabulous!—Stephen

Shopping List

¼ pineapple, peeled, cored and cut into chunks

¼ Granny Smith apple, cored and cut into chunks

6 mint leaves

4 basil leaves

⅛ medium red onion, peeled

½ teaspoon capers, drained

⅛ teaspoon ground black pepper

¼ teaspoon salt

1 teaspoon honey

1 teaspoon rice wine vinegar

1 Place pineapple, apple, mint, basil, onion, capers, pepper, salt, honey and vinegar into the Ninja 16-oz. chopper bowl with blade in position.

2 Pulse 5 to 6 times. Carefully remove blade.

TIP...
If you don't like capers, simply omit them. For the Ninja 40-oz. bowl, double the recipe.

Salsa Guacamole

Prep: 15 min. **Yield:** 1 cup
16-oz. chopper bowl with blade attachment

Two of my favorite Latin condiments are tomato salsa and guacamole. One day I decided to merge the two. Here is the recipe everyone agrees is sublime.—Andrea

Shopping List

¼ medium red onion, peeled

½ jalapeño pepper, top cut off, seeded and cut in half

1 vine-ripe tomato, quartered

¼ cup loosely packed fresh cilantro leaves

¼ yellow bell pepper, cored, and cut into chunks

⅛ teaspoon red pepper flakes

2 tablespoons fresh lime juice

1 ripe avocado, pitted, peeled and cut in chunks

1 Place onion, jalapeño, tomato, cilantro, pepper, pepper flakes, lime juice and avocado into the Ninja 16-oz. chopper bowl with blade in position.

2 Pulse 5 to 7 times. Carefully remove blade.

3 For a creamier version, process until completely smooth.

TIP...

If you don't like spicy food, omit red pepper flakes and jalapeño pepper. For the Ninja 40-oz. bowl, double the recipe.

Guacamole

Prep: 8 min. **Yield:** 1½ cups
16-oz. chopper bowl with blade attachment

A staple in Latin cuisine, guacamole is not only great as a dip but also as a sandwich spread, salad topping and as a condiment to top grilled meats.—Andrea

Shopping List

3 cherry tomatoes

1 jalapeño pepper, top cut off, seeded and cut into chunks

½ cup loosely packed cilantro leaves

2 tablespoons lime juice

¼ teaspoon ground black pepper

½ teaspoon salt

2 ripe avocados, peeled, pitted and cut into chunks

1 Place tomatoes, jalapeño, cilantro, lime juice, black pepper, salt and avocados into the Ninja 16-oz. chopper bowl with blade in position.

2 Pulse 5 to 7 times. Carefully remove blade.

3 For creamy guacamole, process until completely smooth.

TIP...

If you like garlic in your guacamole, add a small peeled clove of garlic with all the other ingredients. For the Ninja 40-oz. bowl, double the recipe.

Hummus

Prep: 15 min. **Yield:** 3½ cups
40-oz. bowl with blade attachment

There is no better snack when you are on a diet, than having hummus with fresh raw vegetables. Full of fiber and protein, it will keep you full without consuming too many calories.—Bob

Shopping List

2 (15½-ounce) cans garbanzo beans, drained and rinsed

3 tablespoons tahini

¼ cup plus 2 tablespoons freshly squeezed lemon juice

¾ teaspoon salt

¾ teaspoon ground black pepper

¼ cup extra virgin olive oil

¼ teaspoon cayenne pepper

3 cloves garlic, peeled

¼ cup cold water

1 Place beans, tahini, lemon juice, salt, black pepper, oil, cayenne pepper, garlic and water into the Ninja 40-oz. bowl with blade in position.

2 Pulse 10 times then process until creamy. Carefully remove blade.

TIP...
If you are not a garlic fan, just omit it. Spread hummus on your bread when making a vegetarian sandwich to get some extra protein.

Edamame Hummus

Prep: 15 min. **Yield:** 3¾ cups
40-oz. bowl with blade attachment

Typically found in the cuisines of Japan, China and Hawaii, edamame are soy beans full of protein that pack a nutritional punch. These great beans make a terrific dip.—Andrea

Shopping List

1 pound shelled edamame soy beans, cooked

¾ cup nonfat Greek yogurt

1 teaspoon ground coriander

2 tablespoons lower sodium soy sauce

1 tablespoon sesame oil

¼ cup cold water

3 cloves garlic, peeled

¼ cup freshly squeezed lemon juice

1¼ teaspoons ground black pepper

1 Place edamame, yogurt, coriander, soy sauce, oil, water, garlic, lemon juice and pepper into the Ninja 40-oz. bowl with blade in position.

2 Process until creamy, about 1 minute. Carefully remove blade.

TIP...
Edamame are typically found in your supermarket freezer in whole pods or shelled. Follow the instructions on the package to cook.

BOB WARDEN

Bob Warden

Bob Warden is a renowned television cooking celebrity, kitchenware developer and cookbook author. His newest venture, Great Chefs International, includes a TV show and a variety of new cookbooks as well as the premiere of Great Flavors®, a collection of concentrated stocks, sauces and seasonings. In a highly productive print career, Bob has published eight customer-top-rated, five-star cookbooks. They include *Quick and Easy Pressure Cooking*, *The Ninja Master Prep Cookbook*, *The Ninja Master Prep Professional Cookbook*, *The Ultimate Bulk Buying Cookbook*, *Best of the Best Cook's Essentials Cookbook*, and *Bob Warden's Slow Food Fast*, which has sold more than 200,000 copies. Selling more than 150,000 copies in its first year, Bob's newest pressure cooker cookbook, *Great Food Fast*, has become the ultimate go-to-reference for pressure cooking. It has the distinction of being 2012's fifth best-selling cookbook in the nation.

Stephen Delaney

Philadelphia born and raised, Stephen Delaney graduated from Johnson & Wales University, Providence, Rhode Island. His twenty-year career as a chef has taken him to top venues, including the Ritz Carlton, Naples Grande Resort, Doubletree by Hilton, and the Doral Country Club. In 2000, his chili was named the best in the United States by *Parade Magazine*. His writings on food have appeared in more than forty newspapers and magazines. Stephen's style of cuisine is a unique combination of Caribbean, Italian, Spanish and Asian.

Andrea Schwob

A native of Caracas, Venezuela, Andrea Schwob first earned a law degree, then came to the United States to pursue her true passion, the culinary arts. She graduated from Florida Culinary Institute in West Palm Beach with an International Baking and Pastry degree. She has worked at Polo Club in Boca Raton, Florida, Roy's Restaurant, Naples Grande Resort, Cosimo Restaurant in Malvern, Pennsylvania, and finally at QVC for the last five years as a food stylist. During most of that time, she has also been the stylist for the over 500,000 Ninja Kitchen Systems sold on QVC. She has won numerous pastry awards and has been widely featured in television and print media.

Index

Notes

Notes

Notes